100 PROGRAMS
FOR THE
AMSTRAD 464, 664 AND 6128

100 PROGRAMS
FOR THE
AMSTRAD 464, 664 AND 6128

Ian McLean
John Gordon
MEDC, Paisley College, Scotland

Prentice/Hall International

Englewood Cliffs, NJ   London   Mexico   New Delhi   Rio de Janeiro
Singapore   Sydney   Tokyo   Toronto   Wellington

AMSTRAD is a trademark of Amstrad Consumer Electronics plc

British Library Cataloguing in Publication Data

McLean, Ian, 1946-
  100 programs for the Amstrad.—(Prentice-Hall
  International personal computer book)
  1. Amstrad Microcomputer—Programming
  I. Title   II. Gordon, John, 1952-
  001.64'25   QA76.8.A4

ISBN 0-13-635004-6

Library of Congress Cataloging-in-Publication Data

McLean, Ian, 1946-
    100 programs for the Amstrad CPC 464, 664, and 6128
    1. Amstrad Microcomputer – Programming.
I. Gordon, John, 1952-   .II. Title. III. Title.
One hundred programs for the Amstrad CPC 464, 664 and 6128.
QA76.8.A48M33 1986   005.36   85-19415
ISBN 0-13-635004-6 (pbk.)

ISBN 0-13-635004-6

PRENTICE-HALL INC., Englewood Cliffs, New Jersey
PRENTICE-HALL INTERNATIONAL (UK) LTD., London
PRENTICE-HALL OF AUSTRALIA PTY., Ltd., Sydney
PRENTICE-HALL CANADA, INC., Toronto
PRENTICE-HALL HISPANOAMERICANA, S.A., Mexico
PRENTICE-HALL OF INDIA PRIVATE LIMITED, New Delhi
PRENTICE-HALL OF JAPAN, INC., Tokyo
PRENTICE-HALL OF SOUTHEAST ASIA PTE., LTD., Singapore

Printed in the United Kingdom by A. Wheaton & Co Ltd., Exeter
10 9 8 7

Contents

Section 6—Data Handling

Section 7—Recreation

Section 8—For The School

Section 9—Science Lab

Section 10—Mathematics

Introduction

It is with a sense of satisfaction that we present to you this selection of computer programs for your Amstrad.

We have, in our selection, attempted to answer the question:

"What do you use a microcomputer for?"

You will find routines in this book which cover the use of a micro at home, in business, at school and for pleasure.

The programs in the selection are laid out in the following format:

Program commentary.
Program listing.
On occasion a photograph of the screen or a printout.

The programs themselves exhibit many styles of construction and more than one style of presentation.

Some of the programs are almost totally "user-friendly" and some are quite terse. Some of the programs are well littered with commentary lines and some are quite sparse.

We have, in our programs, shown off the machine as far as we could.

All the programs in this book have been written so that they will run, without modification, on the CPC 464 with datarecorder, on the CPC 464 with additional disk drive and on the CPC 664. An option available to those with access to disk storage is to save data as it is entered, rather than storing it in an array and saving at the end of data entry, as is dane in the file handling programs in this book. Modifying these programs to use this alternative method could be a useful exercise. Cassette users may wish to add to programs, where relevant, reminders to rewind the tape to the start of a file before loading and after saving.

We must mention at this point the possibility of bugs. It is possible that we have left a few in the code. Hopefully, through the efforts of Prentice-Hall in carrying out field tests, these will be at a minimum. If there are any left, then we take this opportunity to apologise for them.

In a sense, however, none of these programs is complete.
They could all be expanded in various ways. One of the joys
of computing is to take a simple routine and give it a
professional user-friendly appearance. We have not attempted
to make our programs complete in this sense. This is left up
to you. Consider this book to form part of your software
library.

P1 Dice

A gambler's delight, this program rolls three dice.

This could be extended into a game where you bet against the computer.

COMMANDS

Key in the program and RUN.
The space bar rolls the dice.
Key S stops the program.

```
10 REM Dice
20 MODE 0
30 PEN 1
40 BORDER 1
50 PAPER 0
60 s$=SPACE$(18)
70 r$=CHR$(129)
80 t$=CHR$(32)
90 :
100 REM Put dot patterns in strings
110 a$=r$+t$+t$
120 b$=t$+r$+t$
130 c$=t$+t$+r$
140 d$=r$+t$+r$
150 e$=t$+t$+t$
160 :
170 LOCATE 2,1
180 PRINT "This program rolls"
190 PRINT TAB(2)"three dice."
200 DIM dc$(3,3)
210 :
220 WHILE k$<>"s" AND k$<>"S"
230 :   LOCATE 4,22
240 :   PRINT "Space to roll"
250 :   LOCATE 4,24
260 :   PRINT "Key S to stop
270 :   k$=INKEY$:IF k$="" THEN 270
280 :   LOCATE 1,12
290 :   PRINT s$
300 :   PRINT s$
310 :   PRINT s$
320 :
330 :   FOR n=1 TO 3
340 :     vl%=1+6*RND(1)
350 :     ON vl% GOSUB 520,580,640,700,760,820,820
360 :   NEXT
370 :
380 :   LOCATE 1,12
```

```
390 :    FOR n=1 TO 3
400 :       PRINT e$;dc$(1,n);e$;dc$(2,n);e$;dc$(3,n)
410 :    NEXT
420 :
430 :    FOR k=0 TO 200:NEXT
440 WEND
450 MODE 1
460 END
470 :
480 :
490 REM Subroutines
500 :
510 ren One
520 dc$(n,1)=e$
530 dc$(n,2)=b$
540 dc$(n,3)=e$
550 RETURN
560 :
570 ren Two
580 dc$(n,1)=a$
590 dc$(n,2)=e$
600 dc$(n,3)=c$
610 RETURN
620 :
630 REM Three
640 dc$(n,1)=a$
650 dc$(n,2)=b$
660 dc$(n,3)=c$
670 RETURN
680 :
690 REM Four
700 dc$(n,1)=d$
710 dc$(n,2)=e$
720 dc$(n,3)=d$
730 RETURN
740 :
750 REM five
760 dc$(n,1)=d$
770 dc$(n,2)=b$
780 dc$(n,3)=d$
790 RETURN
800 :
810 REM Six
820 dc$(n,1)=d$
830 dc$(n,2)=d$
840 dc$(n,3)=d$
850 RETURN
```

P2 Musak

This program turns your Amstrad into a musical instrument. The bottom three rows of keys select three octaves. Keys 1 to 9 select note length.

The program gives the simplest possible algorithm for ease of understanding. It can be extended in many ways. For example the three available voices can be used to implement chords; noise can be introduced for special effects; different tone envelopes can be selected.

COMMANDS

Key in the program and RUN.
Stop the program by pressing the RETURN key.


```
10 REM Musak
20 PAPER 0:INK 0,1
30 PEN 1:INK 1,24
40 BORDER 1
50 MODE 1
60 CLS
70 PRINT:PRINT
80 PRINT TAB(16)"-------"
90 PRINT TAB(16)" MUSAK "
100 PRINT TAB(16)"-------"
110 LOCATE 1,8
120 PRINT"This program lets you play the computer"
130 PRINT"like a musical instrument."
140 LOCATE 1,12
150 PRINT"Keys 1 to 9 select note length."
160 PRINT:PRINT
170 PRINT"Keys Q W E R T Y U I O P @ ["
180 PRINT TAB(6)"A S D F G H J K L : ; ]"
190 PRINT TAB(6)"SPACE Z X C V B N M , . / \"
200 PRINT"Select note."
210 PRINT:PRINT
220 PRINT"ENTER Key stops the program."
230 :
240 DIM per(36):REM Note periods
250 FOR n=1 TO 36
260 :   READ per(n)
270 NEXT
280 :
290 kb$(1)="[@poiuytrewq"
300 kb$(2)="];:lkjhgfdsa"
310 kb$(3)="\/.,mnbvcxz"+CHR$(32)
320 :
330 nl=5:REM Default length
340 WHILE a$<>CHR$(13)
350 :   a$=INKEY$:IF LEN(a$)=0 THEN 350
```

```
360 :
370 :    a$=LOWER$(a$)
380 :    IF ASC(a$)>48 AND ASC(a$)<58 THEN nl=ASC(a$)-48
390 :
400 :    found=0
410 :    FOR oct=1 TO 3
420 :      FOR nt=1 TO 12
430 :        IF a$=MID$(KB$(oct),nt,1) THEN GOSUB 580
440 :      NEXT
450 :    NEXT
460 :    IF found=1 THEN SOUND 129,0,1,0:SOUND 1,pr,15+10*nl,7
470 WEND
480 CLS
490 END
500 :
510 :
520 DATA 63,67,71,75,80,84,89,95,100,106,113,119
530 DATA 127,134,142,150,159,169,179,190,201,213,225,239
540 DATA 253,268,284,301,319,338,358,379,402,426,451,478
550 :
560 :
570 REM Set frequency
580 found=1
590 pr=per((oct-1)*12+nt)
600 nt=12
610 oct=3
620 RETURN
```

P3 Bouncing Ball

This program shows a simple method of achieving animation using PRINT instructions. Animation is achieved by placing the ball on the screen and then placing a space on top. The ball is then placed one position on.

COMMANDS

Key in the program and RUN.

```
10 REM Bouncing ball
20 MODE 1
30 DEFINT X,Y,D
40 PAPER 2:INK 2,2
50 PEN 1:INK 1,24
60 BORDER 6
70 CLS
80 S$=SPACE$(1)
90 DX=1
100 DY=1
110 X=3+35*RND(1)
120 Y=3+20*RND(1)
130 :
140 WHILE LEN(a$)=0
150 :   LOCATE X,Y
160 :   PRINT CHR$(181)
170 :   IF X=1 OR X=40 THEN GOSUB 330
180 :   IF Y=1 OR Y=25 THEN GOSUB 380
190 :   LOCATE X,Y
200 :   PRINT S$
210 :   IF X=40 AND Y=25 THEN LOCATE 40,23:PRINT s$
220 :   REM Deletes scroll up effect
230 :   X=X+DX
240 :   Y=Y+DY
250 :   a$=INKEY$:REM press any key to end
260 WEND
270 DEFREAL X,Y,D
280 CLS
290 END
300 :
310 :
320 REM End bounce
330 DX=-DX
340 SOUND 1,0,5,5,0,0,5
350 RETURN
360 :
370 REM Top or bottom bounce
380 DY=-DY
390 SOUND 1,0,5,5,0,0,5
400 RETURN
```

P4   Ball and Wall

This is an extension of the Bouncing Ball program.   One   of
two alternative bounce angles may   be   chosen,   depending   on
whether the ball hits the face or the corner of a brick.   You
could expand this program by introducing a bat to control the
ball and having several layers of wall.

COMMANDS

Key in the program and RUN.


```
10 REM Ball and wall
20 MODE 1
30 DEFINT X,Y,D
40 PAPER 0:INK 0,2:CLS
50  FOR X=624 TO 639
60  :  PLOT X,0
70  :  DRAWR 0,399
80  NEXT
90 :
100 GOSUB 490:REM Wall
110 PEN 1:INK 1,24
120 BORDER 24
130 S$=SPACE$(1)
140 DX=1
150 DY=1
160 X=3+25*RND(1)
170 Y=3+20*RND(1)
180 :
190 WHILE LEN(a$)=0
200 :  LOCATE X,Y
210 :  PRINT CHR$(231)
220 :  IF X=29 OR X=31 THEN GOSUB 570 ELSE flag=0
230 :  IF X=1 OR X=39 OR flag=1 THEN GOSUB 390
240 :  IF Y=1 OR Y=25 THEN GOSUB 440
250 :  LOCATE X,Y
260 :  PRINT S$
270 :  IF X=40 AND Y=25 THEN LOCATE 40,23:PRINT S$
280 :  REM Deletes scroll up effect
290 :  X=X+DX
300 :  Y=Y+DY
310 :  a$=INKEY$:REM press any key to end
320 WEND
330 DEFREAL X,Y,D
340 CLS
350 END
360 :
370 :
380 REM End or wall bounce
390 DX=-DX
400 SOUND 1,0,2+20*flag,5,0,0,5
```

```
410 RETURN
420 :
430 REM Top or bottom bounce
440 DY=-DY
450 SOUND 1,0,2+20*flag,5,0,0,5
460 RETURN
470 :
480 REM Wall
490 PEN 2:INK 2,6
500 FOR Y=1 TO 25
510 :   LOCATE 30,Y
520 :   PRINT CHR$(143)
530 NEXT
540 RETURN
550 :
560 REM Test
570 flag=0
580 IF X=29 AND DX=-1 THEN RETURN
590 IF X=31 AND DX=1 THEN RETURN
600 IF TEST(472,(26-Y)*16-8)=2 THEN GOSUB 660
610 IF Y=0 OR Y=25 THEN RETURN
620 IF TEST(472,(26-Y-DY)*16-8)=2 THEN GOSUB 720
630 RETURN
640 :
650 REM Face
660 flag=1
670 LOCATE 30,Y
680 PRINT S$
690 RETURN
700 :
710 REM Corner
720 IF flag=1 THEN RETURN
730 flag=1
740 LOCATE 30,Y+DY
750 PRINT S$
760 DY=-DY
770 RETURN
```

P5 Digital Clock

This program uses the micro's internal timer to run a 24 hour digital clock. It could be extended to show (say) New York time, Hong Kong time and Greenwich Mean Time in three separate displays.

COMMANDS

Key in the program and RUN.
Enter the current time.


```
10 REM Digital clock
20 INK 0,1
30 INK 1,24
40 PAPER 0
50 PEN 1
60 BORDER 1
70 MODE 1
80 ON BREAK GOSUB 630
90 :
100 a$(0)="Hour (0 - 23)"
110 a$(1)="Minute (0 - 59)"
120 a$(2)="Second (0 - 59)"
130 :
140 FOR n=0 TO 2
150 :   IF n=0 THEN mx=23 ELSE mx=59
160 :   tm(n)=-1
170 :   GOSUB 510
180 NEXT
190 :
200 MODE 0
210 LOCATE 6,8
220 PRINT".........."
230 LOCATE 6,11
240 PRINT".........."
250 start=INT(TIME/300)
260 WHILE tm(0)<24
270 :   WHILE tm(1)<60
280 :     sec=tm(2)
290 :     WHILE tm(2)<60
300 :       tm(2)=sec+INT(TIME/300)-start
310 :       LOCATE 6,10
320 :       PRINT":";
330 :       FOR n=0 TO 2
340 :         tm$(n)=MID$(STR$(tm(n)),2)
350 :         IF LEN(tm$(n))=1 THEN tm$(n)="0"+tm$(n)
360           PRINT tm$(n);":";
370           NEXT
380 :     WEND
390 :     start=start+60-sec
400 :     tm(1)=tm(1)+1
```

```
410 :      tm(2)=0
420 :   WEND
430 :   tm(0)=tm(0)+1
440 :   IF tm(0)=24 THEN tm(0)=0
450 :   tm(1)=0
460 WEND
470 END
480 :
490 :
500 REM Get current time
510 WHILE tm(n)<0 OR tm(n)>mx
520 :   CLS
530 :   PRINT TAB(13)"DIGITAL CLOCK"
540 :   PRINT TAB(13)"+++++++++++++"
550 :   LOCATE 1,6
560 :   PRINT a$(n);
570 :   INPUT tm(n)
580 :   WEND
590 RETURN
600 :
610 :
620 REM Press ESC key twice to end program.
630 MODE 1
640 END
```

P6 Jimmy

In this program user defined characters are used to create the cartoon character Jimmy.

We have included a few lines in the program to draw Jimmy and make him wave. These lines are merely an example of how Jimmy can be drawn and moved. You can generate different movements using the shapes given, or expand the program further by defining new shapes.

COMMANDS

Key in the program and RUN.
Stop the program by pressing any key.
Key in your own routines in lines to make Jimmy move.


```
10 REM Jimmy
20 MODE 0
30 BORDER 15
40 PAPER 0
50 INK 0,1
60 CLS
70 PEN 1
80 INK 1,24
90 LOCATE 5,4
100 PRINT"Hello Jimmy!"
110 :
120 REM Define shapes
130 SYMBOL AFTER 240
140 :
150 REM Head
160 SYMBOL 240,24,60,90,126,126,102,62,24
170 :
180 REM Upper trunk
190 SYMBOL 241,24,255,255,255,231,126,102,126
200 :
210 REM Lower trunk
220 SYMBOL 242,102,60,60,60,126,231,231,231
230 :
240 REM Upper left arm
250 SYMBOL 243,0,128,192,224,112,48,48,48
260 :
270 REM Lower left arm
280 SYMBOL 244,48,48,48,0,0,0,0,0
290 :
300 REM Upper right arm
310 SYMBOL 245,0,1,3,7,14,12,12,12
320 :
330 REM Lower right arm
340 SYMBOL 246,12,12,12,0,0,0,0,0
350 :
```

```
360 REM Raise upper left arm
370 SYMBOL 247,0,0,0,48,48,48,48,48
380 :
390 REM Raise lower left arm
400 SYMBOL 248,112,240,192,128,0,0,0,0
410 :
420 REM Legs at attention
430 SYMBOL 249,231,231,231,231,231,231,231,231
440 :
450 REM Left foot
460 SYMBOL 250,0,0,0,0,0,0,192,192
470 :
480 REM Right foot
490 SYMBOL 251,0,0,0,0,0,0,3,3
500 :
510 REM Hat
520 SYMBOL 252,0,0,0,36,60,60,255,255
530 :
540 REM ball
550 SYMBOL 253,0,24,60,126,126,60,24,0
560 :
570 REM Bat
580 SYMBOL 254,60,126,255,126,60,24,24,24
590 :
600 :
610 REM Use the shapes to write your own routines.
620 :
630 REM A sample routine is given.
640 :
650 REM This makes Jimmy wave.
660 :
670 :
680 PEN 2:INK 2,16
690 LOCATE 11,10
700 PRINT CHR$(240)
710 :
720 PEN 3:INK 3,6
730 LOCATE 10,11
740 PRINT CHR$(245);CHR$(241);CHR$(243)
750 :
760 LOCATE 10,12
770 PRINT CHR$(246);CHR$(32);CHR$(244)
780 PEN 4:INK 4,21
790 LOCATE 11,12
800 PRINT CHR$(242)
810 :
820 PEN 5:INK 5,0
830 LOCATE 10,13
840 PRINT CHR$(251);CHR$(249);CHR$(250)
850 :
860 REM Wave
870 PEN 3
880 WHILE LEN(a$)=0
890 :    LOCATE 12,11
900 :    PRINT CHR$(243)
910 :    LOCATE 12,12
920 :    PRINT CHR$(244)
```

```
930 :   FOR k=0 TO 200:NEXT
940 :   LOCATE 12,12
950 :   PRINT CHR$(32)
960 :   LOCATE 12,10
970 :   PRINT CHR$(247)
980 :   LOCATE 12,11
990 :   PRINT CHR$(248)
1000 :  FOR k=0 TO 200:NEXT
1010 :  LOCATE 12,10
1020 :  PRINT CHR$(32)
1030 :  a$=INKEY$:REM Any key to end
1040 WEND
1050 PEN 1
1060 MODE 1
1070 END
```

P7 Runner

This program demonstrates how animation may **be** created by printing one shape over another. The runner is two character spaces wide and is moved forward one space at a time, giving a reasonably continuous motion.

In this program only two figure positions are used. More intermediate positions would give smoother motion.

COMMANDS

Key in the program and RUN.

```
10 REM Runner
20 PAPER 0:INK 0,26
30 PEN 1:INK 1,3
40 BORDER 6
50 MODE 0
60 :
70 SYMBOL 240,0,0,0,0,1,1,1,0
80 SYMBOL 241,6,14,15,14,248,112,127,240
90 SYMBOL 242,1,15,48,32,32,0,0,0
100 SYMBOL 243,252,4,7,0,0,0,0,0
110 SYMBOL 244,0,0,0,0,0,0,0,1
120 SYMBOL 245,0,0,0,0,6,14,207,238
130 SYMBOL 246,1,0,7,7,118,30,1,1
140 SYMBOL 247,120,240,240,220,0,0,0,192
150 :
160 rn1$=CHR$(240)+CHR$(241)
170 rn2$=CHR$(242)+CHR$(243)
180 rn3$=CHR$(244)+CHR$(245)
190 rn4$=CHR$(246)+CHR$(247)
200 :
210 WHILE LEN(a$)=0
220 :   FOR X=1 TO 19 STEP 2
230 :      LOCATE X,15
240 :      PRINT rn1$
250 :      LOCATE X,16
260 :      PRINT rn2$
270 :      FOR n=1 TO 100:NEXT
280 :      LOCATE X,15
290 :      PRINT SPACE$(2)
300 :      LOCATE X,16
310 :      PRINT SPACE$(2)
320 :      IF X=19 THEN 420:REM Screen edge
330 :      LOCATE X+1,15
340 :      PRINT rn3$
350 :      LOCATE X+1,16
360 :      PRINT rn4$
370 :      FOR n=1 TO 100:NEXT
```

```
380 :     LOCATE X+1,15
390 :     PRINT SPACE$(2)
400 :     LOCATE X+1,16
410 :     PRINT SPACE$(2)
420 :   NEXT
430 :   a$=INKEY$
440 :   FOR n=1 TO 100:NEXT
450 WEND
460 MODE 1
470 END
```

P8 Worm

In this program pixels are inked in at the front of a
squiggly shape and deleted behind it. As a result a little
worm slithers across the screen.

COMMANDS

Key in the program and RUN.


```
10 REM Worm
20 BORDER 26
30 PAPER 0:INK 0,0
40 PEN 1:INK 1,24
50 PEN 2:INK 2,20
60 MODE 1
70 :
80 WHILE LEN(a$)=0
90 :   cl=1
100 :    FOR n=1 TO 720
110 :      X=n:IF X>640 THEN X=640
120 :      R=n-80:IF R<0 THEN R=0
130 :      Y=INT(200+15*SIN(X/6))
140 :      W=INT(200+15*SIN(R/6))
150 :      If n/4=INT(n/4) THEN cl=cl+1
160 :      IF cl=3 THEN cl=1
170 :      PLOT X,Y,cl
180 :      PLOT R,W,0
190 :    NEXT
200 :    a$=INKEY$:REM Any key to end
210 WEND
220 :
230 PEN 1
240 CLS
250 END
```

P9 String Pattern

This program generates patterns of straight lines reminiscent of 'pin pictures'. It first obtains the end points of the reference lines and the number of points per line. The equations of the lines in the form $y=m*x+c$ are calculated, followed by the step sizes.

The program then steps down each line, drawing straight lines to produce a pattern thus:

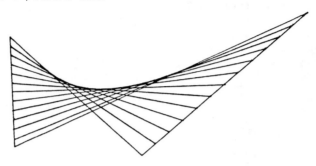

COMMANDS

Key in the program and RUN.
Enter information as requested.


```
10 REM String pattern
20 PAPER 0:INK 0,1
30 PEN 1:INK 1,24
40 BORDER 1
50 MODE 1
60 DIM X%(4)
70 DIM Y%(4)
80 :
90 FOR n=1 TO 4
100 :   WHILE X%(n)<1 OR X%(n)>639
110 :      GOSUB 660:REM Line and point
120 :      INPUT "X-coordinate (1 to 639)";X%(n)
130 :   WEND
140 :
150 :   WHILE Y%(n)<1 OR Y%(n)>399
160 :      GOSUB 660:REM Line and point
170 :      INPUT "Y-coordinate (1 to 399)";Y%(n)
180 :   WEND
190 NEXT
200 :
210 WHILE N%<2
220 :   CLS
230 :   LOCATE 1,4
```

```
240 :   INPUT"Number of points (2 or more)";N%
250 WEND
260 :
270 N%=N%-1
280 IF X%(1)=X%(2) THEN X%(2)=X%(2)+1
290 IF X%(3)=X%(4) THEN X%(4)=X%(4)+1
300 DX1=(X%(2)-X%(1))/N%
310 DX2=(X%(4)-X%(3))/N%
320 M1=(Y%(2)-Y%(1))/(X%(2)-X%(1))
330 M2=(Y%(4)-Y%(3))/(X%(4)-X%(3))
340 B1=Y%(1)-M1*X%(1)
350 B2=Y%(3)-M2*X%(3)
360 :
370 MODE 2
380 CLS
390 PLOT X%(1),Y%(1)
400 DRAW X%(2),Y%(2)
410 PLOT X%(3),Y%(3)
420 DRAW X%(4),Y%(4)
430 :
440 FOR k=0 TO N%
450 :   CX1=X%(1)+k*DX1
460 :   CY1=M1*(X%(1)+k*DX1)+B1
470 :   CX2=X%(4)-k*DX2
480 :   CY2=M2*(X%(4)-k*DX2)+B2
490 :   PLOT CX1,CY1
500 :   DRAW CX2,CY2
510 NEXT
520 :
530 WHILE LEN(a$)=0
540 :   a$=INKEY$
550 WEND
560 IF a$=CHR$(32) THEN RUN
570 REM Space bar for new pattern
580 :
590 REM Any other key to end
600 MODE 1
610 CLS
620 END
630 :
640 :
650 REM Print line and point number
660 CLS
670 LOCATE 15,4
680 IF n<3 THEN PRINT"First line" ELSE PRINT"Second line"
690 LOCATE 15,8
700 IF n=1 OR n=3 THEN PRINT"First point" ELSE PRINT"Second poin·
710 LOCATE 1,16
720 RETURN
```

P10 Guess the Number

In this game the computer generates a random whole number between 1 and 100 and the player has to guess what it is.

The instuctions for the game are included in the code. Remember to press the RETURN key after typing in your guess.

COMMANDS

Key in the program and RUN.

```
100 REM Program - Guess The Number
110 MODE 1
120 PRINT:PRINT:PRINT
130 PRINT "In this program you attempt to "
140 PRINT "outguess the computer.  You will be"
150 PRINT "prompted to guess a number between"
160 PRINT "0 and 100.  If you guess wrongly"
170 PRINT "the computer will tell you if you are"
180 PRINT "too low or too high.  When finished"
190 PRINT "the computer will give you your"
200 PRINT "average number of attempts to "
210 PEN 2
220 PRINT:PRINT:PRINT
230 PRINT "     GUESS THE NUMBER"
240 PEN 1
250 PRINT:PRINT:PRINT
260 PRINT "Press any key to start"
270 z$=INKEY$:IF z$="" THEN 270
280 :
290 MODE 0
300 goes=0
310 attempts=0
320 :
330 a$="Y"
340 WHILE a$="Y" OR a$="y"
350     CLS
360     goes=goes+1
370     number=INT(RND(TIME)*100)
380     correct=0
390     :
400     WHILE NOT correct
410         PEN 1
420         LOCATE 1,12:PRINT "Enter a guess ";
430         INPUT guess
440         CLS
450         IF guess<number THEN PEN 2:LOCATE 1,12:
            PRINT "TOO LOW"
460         IF guess>number THEN PEN 3:LOCATE 1,12:
            PRINT "TOO HIGH"
```

```
470        IF guess=number THEN PEN 4:LOCATE 1,12:
           PRINT "CORRECT":correct=-1
480        FOR i=1 TO 500:NEXT i
490        attempts=attempts+1
500    WEND
510    :
520    CLS
530    LOCATE 1,12:INPUT "Another go (Y/N) ",a$
540 WEND
550 :
560 CLS
570 average=attempts/goes
580 LOCATE 1,12:PRINT "You took an average of ";average;"per shot"
590 IF average<7 THEN LOCATE 1,15:PRINT "PRETTY GOOD"
600 END
```

P11 Reaction Test

This program could help develop your keyboard skills. The computer places a random character on the screen and starts to time your response.

The object of the game is to press the required key as quickly as possible.

When the program is complete an average reaction time is displayed on the screen.

COMMANDS

Key in the program and RUN.

```
100 REM Program - Reaction Test
110 MODE 1
120 BORDER 6:INK 2,17:INK 1,0:PAPER 2:CLS
130 LOCATE 12,2:PRINT "REACTION TEST"
140 LOCATE 6,6:PRINT "How many tries do you want";
150 INPUT no.of.attempts
160 LOCATE 6,8:PRINT "Press any key to start";
170 z$=INKEY$:IF z$="" THEN 170
180 MODE 0
190 FOR letter=1 TO no.of.attempts
200    CLS
210    t=TIME
220    x=INT(RND(6)*20)+1:y=INT(RND(6)*25)+1
230    a$=CHR$(INT(RND(6)*26)+65)
240    LOCATE x,y:PRINT a$
250    b$=UPPER$(INKEY$):IF b$<>a$ THEN 250
260    tot.time=tot.time+(TIME-t)
270 NEXT letter
280 :
290 MODE 1:CLS
300 LOCATE 1,10:PRINT "Number of attemts ";
    USING "#####.##";no.of.attempts
310 PRINT "Total time ";USING "#####.##";tot.time/300;
315 PRINT " seconds"
320 PRINT "Average reaction time was ";USING "##.##";
    tot.time/no.of.attempts/300;
325 PRINT " seconds"
330 END
```

P12 Mastermind

This program implements the first version of the popular game by Invicta Ltd.

The object of the game is to determine the colour of four rectangles on the screen. The player has up to twenty attempts to work out the code.

When an attempt has been entered, the computer responds by indicating whether you have a correctly coloured rectangle in the correct position, or a correctly coloured rectangle in the wrong position.

For each correct colour in the correct position, the computer places a purple dash to the right of the guess.

For each correct colour in the wrong position the computer places a cyan dash to the right of the guess.

COMMANDS

Key in the program and RUN.
Enter your guess as e.g. RGYB.


```
100 REM Program - MasterMind
110 MODE 0
120 DIM colour(3),guess(3),temp(3)
130 SYMBOL 244,0,255,255,255,255,255,255,255
140 Lne=0
150 INK 1,6:INK 2,18:INK 3,24:INK 4,2:INK 5,8:INK 6,10
160 BORDER 16:PAPER 10:CLS
170 LOCATE 2,1:PRINT CHR$(244)+" "+CHR$(244)+" "+
                    CHR$(244)+" "+CHR$(244)
180 FOR i=0 TO 3
190    colour(i)=FIX(RND(TIME)*3)+1
200    temp(i)=colour(i)
210 NEXT i
220 :
230 WHILE pc<>4 AND Lne<>20
240    Lne=Lne+1
250    FOR i=0 TO 3
260       colour(i)=temp(i)
270    NEXT i
280    :
290    PEN 7
300    LOCATE 1,25:INPUT "Enter code ";patt$
310    patt$=UPPER$(patt$)
320    LOCATE 1,25:PRINT SPACE$(20);
330    :
340    FOR i=0 TO 3
```

```
350        guess(i)=0
360        IF MID$(patt$,i+1,1)="R" THEN guess(i)=1
370        IF MID$(patt$,i+1,1)="G" THEN guess(i)=2
380        IF MID$(patt$,i+1,1)="Y" THEN guess(i)=3
390        IF MID$(patt$,i+1,1)="B" THEN guess(i)=4
400        PEN guess(i)
410        LOCATE 2+i*2,lne+1:PRINT CHR$(244);
420      NEXT i
430 :
440      pc=0:cc=0
450      FOR i=0 TO 3
460        IF guess(i)=colour(i) THEN pc=pc+1:colour(i)=10:
                                        guess(i)=11
470      NEXT i
480      :
490      FOR i=0 TO 3
500        FOR j=0 TO 3
510          IF guess(i)=colour(j) THEN cc=cc+1:
                                          colour(j)=10:j=3
520        NEXT j
530      NEXT i
540      :
550      IF pc=0 THEN 590
560      PEN 5
570      FOR i=1 TO pc:LOCATE 10+i*2,lne+1:
         PRINT CHR$(244);:NEXT i
580      :
590      IF cc=0 THEN 630
600      PEN 6
610      FOR i=1 TO cc:LOCATE 10+pc*2+i*2,lne+1:
         PRINT CHR$(244);:NEXT i
620      :
630 WEND
640 PEN 7
650 :
660 IF pc<>4 THEN 740
670 z=TIME
680 WHILE ((TIME-z)/300)<5:WEND
690 CLS
700 LOCATE 1,13:PRINT "WELL DONE!!!"
710 PRINT:PRINT:PRINT
720 PRINT "You took ";lne;" attempts"
730 GOTO 820
740 CLS
750 LOCATE 1,10:PRINT "The correct code was:"
760 :
770 FOR i=0 TO 3
780   PEN temp(i)
790   LOCATE 10+i*2,12:PRINT CHR$(244);
800 NEXT i
810 PRINT
820 END
```

P13 Gobble

In this program we show the effects of simple graphics.

We have two beasties eating up a field of grass. This is a two player game, with each player taking the part of a beastie.

```
                      W
Player 1 uses keys    A  S
                      Z


                      [
Player 2 uses keys    ;  ]
                      \
```

If a player leaves the field or attempts to eat a patch of grass which has already been eaten, he dies.

Every time grass is eaten, points are scored.

COMMANDS

Key in the program and RUN.


```
100 REM Program - Gobble
110 :
120 REM Set up board
130 MODE 0
140 BORDER 6:INK 1,2:INK 2,18:PAPER 2:CLS
150 :
160 REM Initialise parameters
170 DIM x(2),y(2),dx(2),dy(2),score(2)
180 x(1)=1:x(2)=640:y(1)=200:y(2)=200
190 a=1:b=2
200 flag=0
210 :
220 REM Play game
230 WHILE NOT game.over
240     dy(1)=((INKEY(71)=0)-(INKEY(59)=0))*2
250     dy(2)=((INKEY(22)=0)-(INKEY(17)=0))*2
260     dx(1)=((INKEY(69)=0)-(INKEY(60)=0))*4
270     dx(2)=((INKEY(28)=0)-(INKEY(19)=0))*4
280     FOR i=a TO b
290        IF dx(i)+dy(i)=0 THEN 310
300        IF TEST(x(i)+dx(i),y(i)+dy(i))<>2 THEN
           GOSUB 410 ELSE GOSUB 470
```

```
310     NEXT i
320 WEND
330 :
340 REM Display result
350 MODE 0:CLS
360 LOCATE 1,10:PRINT "Player 1's score is ";score(1)
370 LOCATE 1,14:PRINT "Player 2's score is ";score(2)
380 WHILE INKEY$<>"":WEND
390 END
400 REM Routine to end game
410 PRINT CHR$(7);CHR$(7);CHR$(7)
420 IF i=1 THEN a=2 ELSE b=1
430 flag=flag+1
440 IF flag=2 THEN game.over=-1
450 RETURN
460 REM Routine to move beasty
470 x(i)=x(i)+dx(i)
480 y(i)=y(i)+dy(i)
490 p=(i=1)*-1 + (i=2)*-3
500 DRAW x(i),y(i),p
510 score(i)=score(i)+1
520 RETURN
```

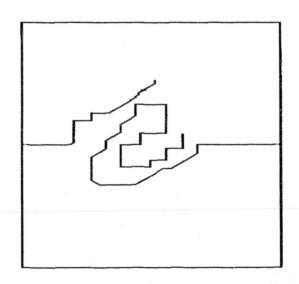

P14 Tennis

This is an adaptation of an old video game. We have two players playing tennis on a green pitch.

Player 1 uses keys Z and X to move his bat.
Player 2 uses keys / and \ to move his bat.

The score is displayed at the top of the screen.

COMMANDS

Key in the program and RUN.
The game does not start until a key is pressed.


```
100 REM Program - Tennis
110 balls.left=10
120 DIM goals(2)
130 INK 2,18:PAPER 2:CLS ' green background
140 SYMBOL 244,0,0,24,60,60,24,0,0
150 SYMBOL 245,24,24,24,24,24,24,24,24
160 ball$=CHR$(244):unball$=" "
170 bat$=CHR$(245)
180 unbat$=" "
190 bx=2:by=19:sped=5
200 LOCATE bx,11:PRINT bat$
210 LOCATE by,11:PRINT bat$
220 player.1=11:player.2=11
230 MODE 0:CLS
240 WHILE INKEY$="":WEND
250 BORDER 6
260 x%=10:y%=13
270 IF RND(6)>0.5 THEN dx%=-1 ELSE dx%=1
280 IF RND(6)>0.5 THEN dy%=-1 ELSE dy%=1
290 PEN 0
300 WHILE balls.left>0
310    m=m+1
320    IF m<sped THEN GOTO 380
330    LOCATE x%,y%:PRINT unball$;
340    x%=x%+dx%:y%=y%+dy%
350    IF y%<2 OR y%>24 THEN dy%=-dy% ' wall bounce
360    LOCATE x%,y%:PRINT ball$;
370    :
380    REM see if bat moves
390    d.player.1=(INKEY(71)=0) - (INKEY(63)=0)
400    d.player.2=(INKEY(30)=0) - (INKEY(22)=0)
410    temp.1=player.1+d.player.1
420    temp.2=player.2+d.player.2
430    IF temp.1<24 AND temp.1>2 THEN LOCATE bx,player.1:
       PRINT unbat$;:LOCATE bx,temp.1:PRINT bat$;:player.1=temp.1
440    IF temp.2<24 AND temp.2>2 THEN LOCATE by,player.2:
       PRINT unbat$;:LOCATE by,temp.2:PRINT bat$;:player.2=temp.2
```

```
450     IF m<sped THEN GOTO 500 ELSE m=1
460     IF x%=by AND y%=player.2 THEN PRINT CHR$(7):
        dx%=-dx%
470     IF x%>by THEN k=1:GOSUB 550
480     IF x%=bx AND y%=player.1 THEN PRINT CHR$(7):
        dx%=-dx%
490     IF x%<bx THEN k=2:GOSUB 550
500 WEND
510 WHILE INKEY$<>"":WEND
520 END
530 REM Wall bounce routine
540 REM Score routine
550    PRINT CHR$(7)
560    balls.left=balls.left-1
570    goals(k)=goals(k)+1
580    LOCATE (k-1)*16+1,1:PRINT USING "##";goals(k)
590    LOCATE x%,y%:PRINT unball$;
600    x%=10
610 RETURN
```

P15 Bombs

In this program, the user has to defend his city against attacks from the sky. The defender can use his laser gun to knock out bombs which appear at random at the top of the screen.

Cursor control keys are used to move the gun and COPY to fire.

COMMANDS

Key in the program and RUN.


```
100 REM Program - Bombs
110 flag=0:f=0
120 MODE 1
130 SYMBOL 244,255,153,153,255,255,129,129,255
140 SYMBOL 245,24,126,231,219,219,231,126,0
150 SYMBOL 246,231,102,60,24,24,24,24,24
160 SYMBOL 247,0,0,0,24,24,0,0,0
170 shell$=CHR$(247)
180 bomb$=CHR$(226)
190 d$=CHR$(245):c$=CHR$(244)
200 c2$=c$+c$
210 c3$=c2$+c$
220 c7$=c3$+c2$+c2$
230 c10$=c7$+c3$
240 c16$=c7$+c7$+c2$
250 c18$=c2$+c16$
260 PEN 1
270 LOCATE 5,19:PRINT c3$+SPACE$(4)+c2$+SPACE$(2)+c3$
    +SPACE$(3)+c3$+SPACE$(4)+c3$
280 PRINT SPACE$(4)+c3$+SPACE$(4)+c2$+SPACE$(2)+c3$+
    SPACE$(3)+c3$+SPACE$(4)+c3$
290 PRINT SPACE$(4)+c3$+" "+c10$+SPACE$(3)+c18$
300 PRINT c7$+" "+c10$+SPACE$(3)+c18$
310 PRINT c7$+" "+c10$+SPACE$(3)+c18$
320 PRINT SPACE$(4)+c3$+" "+c10$+SPACE$(3)+c18$
330 PRINT SPACE$(4)+c3$+" "+c10$+SPACE$(3)+c18$;
340 :
350 a=20
360 b=INT(RND(6)*38)+1
370 z=1
380 MOVE 0,0
390 LOCATE 25,1:PRINT "Bombs landed ";:hit=0
400 LOCATE 1,1:PRINT "Bombs blasted ";:blast=0
410 r=a:s=18
420 :
430 WHILE hit<555
440     LOCATE 35,1:PRINT hit;
```

```
450     fire=(INKEY(9)=0)
460     left=(INKEY(8)=0)
470     right=(INKEY(1)=0)
480     IF fire AND flag=0 THEN flag=1:r=a:PRINT CHR$(7);
490     IF flag=1 THEN LOCATE r,s-1:PRINT shell$;:
        LOCATE r,s:PRINT " ";:GOSUB 640:s=s-1
500     k=left-right+(a=39)-(a=1)
510     LOCATE a,18:PRINT " ";
520     LOCATE a+k,18:PRINT d$;
530     a=a+k
540     g=620*b/40:h=400*(25-z-1)/25
550     q=(TEST(g,h)=1)
560     IF f=1 THEN LOCATE b,z:PRINT " ";:LOCATE b,z+1:
        PRINT bomb$;:z=z+1
570     f=(f+1) MOD 3
580     IF z=24 OR q THEN LOCATE b,z:PRINT " ";:LOCATE b,z+1:
        PRINT " ";:z=2:b=INT(RND(6)*40)+1:hit=hit+1
590 WEND
600 END
610 :
620 :
630 REM Bang routine
640  t=(b=r) AND (s=z+1)
650  IF t THEN SOUND 1,200,10,7,0,0,1:blast=blast+1:LOCATE 14,2:
     PRINT blast;:z=2:b=INT(RND(6)*40)+1
660  IF t OR s=3 THEN flag=0:LOCATE r,s-1:PRINT " ":LOCATE r,s:
     PRINT " ":PRINT " ";:r=a:s=19
670 RETURN
```

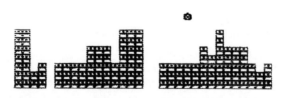

P16 Monster Island

In this program you have landed on a volcanic island and are being pursued by voracious monsters.

Your only hope is to lead the monsters into volcanic pits, over which you can jump.

Use cursor control to move man. Notice that the program can cheat.

COMMANDS

Key in the program and RUN.
Follow instructions.


```
100 REM Program - Monster Island
110 MODE 1:w=40:BORDER 6
120 LOCATE 2,10:INPUT "Speed (1 to 5)";sped:sped=6-sped
130 CLS
140 count=0
150 dead=0
160 m=FIX(RND(TIME)*5)+1:p=FIX(RND(TIME)*5)+3
170 DIM mons(m,2),man(2)
180 el$=" "
190 :
200 SYMBOL 244,31,124,200,248,248,120,60,31      ' Monster
210 SYMBOL 245,60,126,255,254,254,62,30,28       ' Pool
220 SYMBOL 246,28,28,8,127,28,20,20,54           ' Man
230 :
240 FOR i=1 TO m
250    mons(i,1)=FIX(RND(TIME)*w)+1
260    mons(i,2)=FIX(RND(TIME)*25)+1
270    PEN 1
280    LOCATE mons(i,1),mons(i,2):PRINT CHR$(244);
290 NEXT i
300 :
310 FOR i=1 TO p
320    x=FIX(RND(TIME)*w)+1
330    y=FIX(RND(TIME)*25)+1
340    PEN 3
350    LOCATE x,y:PRINT CHR$(245);
360 NEXT i
370 :
380 man(1)=FIX(RND(TIME)*w)+1
390 man(2)=FIX(RND(TIME)*25)+1
400 dx=0:dy=0
410 PEN 2
420 LOCATE man(1),man(2):PRINT CHR$(246);
430 WHILE INKEY$="":WEND
440 :
```

```
450 WHILE m>0 AND NOT dead
460     PEN 2
470     LOCATE man(1),man(2):PRINT CHR$(246);
480     dx=(INKEY(8)=0)-(INKEY(1)=0)
490     dy=(INKEY(0)=0)-(INKEY(2)=0)
500     cx=man(1)+dx:cy=man(2)+dy:GOSUB 710
        'test to see if anything there
510     IF man(1)+dx=40 OR man(1)+dx=1 THEN dx=0
520     IF man(2)+dy=25 OR man(2)+dy=1 THEN dy=0
530     IF c=1 THEN GOSUB 750      'die
540     IF c=3 THEN el$=CHR$(245) ELSE el$=" "
550     IF dx=0 AND dy=0 THEN GOTO 620
560     IF el$=" " THEN PEN 0 ELSE PEN 3
570     LOCATE man(1),man(2):PRINT el$;
580     PEN 2
590     man(1)=man(1)+dx
600     man(2)=man(2)+dy
610     LOCATE man(1),man(2):PRINT CHR$(246);
620     count=(count+1) MOD sped
630     IF count=0 THEN GOSUB 840   'move monsters
640 WEND
650 :
660 WHILE INKEY$<>"":WEND   'flush buffer
670 IF m=0 THEN INK 0,5,8
680 END
690 :
700 REM Routine to examine contents of location
710 c=TEST((cx-1)*16+4,(25-cy)*16+4)
720 RETURN
730 :
740 REM Die procedure
750 INK 0,9,4
760 FOR z=20 TO 0 STEP -1
770   SOUND 1,10+n,100,7
780   WHILE SQ(1)>127:WEND
790 NEXT z
800 dead=-1
810 RETURN
820 :
830 REM Routine to move monsters
840 FOR i=1 TO m
850   LOCATE mons(i,1),mons(i,2):PRINT " ";
860   x=SGN(man(1)-mons(i,1))
870   y=SGN(man(2)-mons(i,2))
880   cx=mons(i,1)+x:cy=mons(i,2)+y:GOSUB 710
890 LOCATE 1,1:PRINT c
900   IF c=3 THEN GOSUB 990:GOTO 950   'kill monster
910   PEN 1
920   IF c=1 THEN LOCATE cx,cy:PRINT CHR$(244);:
        GOSUB 750:RETURN   'dead man
930   mons(i,1)=cx:mons(i,2)=cy
940   LOCATE cx,cy:PRINT CHR$(244);
950 NEXT i
960 RETURN
970 :
980 REM Routine to kill monster
990 PRINT CHR$(7);
```

```
1000 LOCATE mons(i,1),mons(i,2):PRINT " ";
1010 IF i=m THEN m=m-1:RETURN
1020 FOR j=i TO m-1
1030    mons(j,1)=mons(j+1,1)
1040    mons(j,2)=mons(j+1,2)
1050 NEXT j
1060 m=m-1
1070 RETURN
```

P17   Bat 'n' Moth

You've heard of bat'n'ball - well here's bat'n'moth. The bat is a composite shape made up from four user defined characters. It may be moved across and up and down the screen by the cursor control keys.

You can specify the level of difficulty. This controls the speed of the moths and the range of the bat. There is a random element in the former. As a result of this, catching the last moth, even at the lower levels of difficulty, can drive you to distraction. You have been warned!!!

COMMANDS

Key in the program and RUN.


```
100 REM Program - Bat'n'Moth
110 DIM x(10),y(10),dx(10),dy(10)
120 MODE 1
130 FOR i=244 TO 249
140    READ b1,b2,b3,b4,b5,b6,b7,b8
150    SYMBOL i,b1,b2,b3,b4,b5,b6,b7,b8
160 NEXT i
170 :
180 REM define characters
190 m1$=CHR$(244):m2$=CHR$(245)
200 bat1$=CHR$(246)+CHR$(247)
210 bat2$=CHR$(248)+CHR$(249)
220 unbat1$="  "
230 unbat2$="  "
240 :
250 REM Select pallette
260 REM ink
270 REM ink
280 :
290 INPUT "Number of moths (1 to 10) ",k:k=k-1
300 k1=k+1
310 :
320 FOR i=0 TO k
330    x(i)=FIX(RND(6)*16)+2
340    dx(i)=1
350    y(i)=FIX(RND(6)*21)+2
360    dy(i)=1
370 NEXT i
380 :
390 INPUT "Difficulty (1 to 5) ",d:d=5-d
400 MODE 0
410 bx=11:by=13
420 LOCATE 11,13:PRINT bat1$;
430 LOCATE 11,14:PRINT bat2$;
440 :
```

```
450 z=TIME
460 :
470 WHILE k>-1
480    FOR i=0 TO k
490       IF x(i)+dx(i)>17 OR x(i)+dx(i)<3
          THEN dx(i)=-dx(i)*2
500       IF y(i)+dy(i)>22 OR y(i)+dy(i)<3
          THEN dy(i)=-dy(i)*2
510       LOCATE x(i),y(i):PRINT m1$
520    NEXT i
530    :
540    GOSUB 820   'manipulate bat
550    :
560    FOR i=0 TO k
570       LOCATE x(i),y(i):PRINT " ";
580       x(i)=x(i)+dx(i):y(i)=y(i)+dy(i)
590       LOCATE x(i),y(i):PRINT m2$;
600    NEXT i
610    :
620    GOSUB 820   'manipulate bat
630    :
640    FOR i=0 TO k
650       LOCATE x(i),y(i):PRINT " ";
660       dx(i)=FIX(RND(TIME)*3)
670       dy(i)=FIX(RND(TIME)*3)
680    NEXT i
690    :
700 WEND
710 :
720 WHILE INKEY$<>"":WEND 'flush buffer
730 :
740 z=(TIME-z)/300/k1   'time per moth secs
750 z=FIX(z*(5-d))
760 MODE 1
770 LOCATE 10,10:PRINT "Score = ";z
780 WHILE INKEY$<>"":WEND 'flush buffer
790 END
800 :
810 REM Manipulate bat subroutine
820 LOCATE bx,by:PRINT unbat1$;
830 LOCATE bx,by+1:PRINT unbat2$;
840 :
850 by=by+(INKEY(0)=0)-(INKEY(2)=0)
860 bx=bx+(INKEY(8)=0)-(INKEY(1)=0)
870 :
880 IF by<2 THEN by=by+1
890 IF by>22 THEN by=by-1
900 :
910 IF bx<2 THEN bx=bx+1
920 IF bx>18 THEN bx=bx-1
930 :
940 LOCATE bx,by:PRINT bat1$;
950 LOCATE bx,by+1:PRINT bat2$;
960 :
970 IF (INKEY(9)=0) THEN GOSUB 1010   'gulp a moth
980 RETURN
990 :
```

```
1000 REM Routine to eat moth
1010 FOR i=0 TO k
1020    IF ABS(bx-x(i))>d OR ABS(by-y(i))>d
        THEN PRINT CHR$(7):GOTO 1100   ' missed
1030    SOUND 1,200,10,7,0,0,1
1040    LOCATE x(i),y(i):PRINT " ";
1050    FOR t=i TO k-1
1060      x(t)=x(t+1)
1070      y(t)=y(t+1)
1080    NEXT t
1090    k=k-1
1100 NEXT i
1110 RETURN
1120 :
1130 :
1140 DATA 129,129,195,231,255,231,195,129
1150 DATA 36,102,102,102,126,102,102,36
1160 DATA 130,130,129,195,199,195,225,227
1170 DATA 65,65,129,195,227,195,135,199
1180 DATA 231,255,255,239,231,197,137,156
1190 DATA 231,255,255,247,231,163,145,57
```

P18 Loan Repayment Period

This program uses the formula

$$T = -\frac{1}{N} * \frac{\log(1-(P.R)/(N.A))}{\log(1+R/N)}$$

where T=Period in years
P=Principal
R=Rate of interest
N=Number of payments each year
A=Amount of each payment.

This could be calculated by using a calculator, but it is far quicker to allow the computer to do the work for you.

COMMANDS

Key in the program and RUN.
Follow instructions.

```
10 REM Loan repayment period
20 PAPER 0:INK 0,1
30 PEN 1:INK 1,24
40 BORDER 1
50 MODE 1
60 :
70 PRINT TAB(10)"--------------------"
80 PRINT TAB(10)"LOAN REPAYMENT PERIOD"
90 PRINT TAB(10)"--------------------"
100 PRINT:PRINT
110 PRINT"This program  calculates  how long  it"
120 PRINT"will take to pay off a loan."
130 PRINT:PRINT
140 PRINT"To use the program you must input:"
150 PRINT
160 PRINT TAB(2)"(1) the amount borrowed"
170 PRINT TAB(2)"(2) the annual interest rate"
180 PRINT TAB(2)"(3) the number of repayments per year"
190 PRINT TAB(2)"(4) the amount of each repayment."
200 PRINT:PRINT:PRINT
210 PRINT"Press any key to continue."
220 a$=INKEY$:IF LEN(a$)=0 THEN 220
230 :
240 CLS
```

```
250 LOCATE 1,8
260 INPUT "Amount borrowed?                 ",p
270 INPUT "Annual interest rate (%)?        ",r
280 INPUT "Number of payments per year";n
290 INPUT "Regular payment amount?          ",a
300 :
310 r=r/100
320 ON ERROR GOTO 510
330 tm=-LOG(1-p*r/n/a)/LOG(1+r/n)/n
340 yr=INT(tm)
350 mt=12*(tm-yr)
360 IF mt<>INT(mt) THEN mt=INT(mt+1)
370 IF mt=12 THEN yr=yr+1:mt=0
380 :
390 PRINT:PRINT:PRINT
400 PRINT TAB(4);"Loan will be paid off in:"
410 PRINT
420 PRINT TAB(3);yr;"year(s) and";mt;"month(s)."
430 PRINT:PRINT:PRINT
440 PRINT"Press any key to end program."
450 a$=INKEY$:IF LEN(a$)=0 THEN 450
460 CLS
470 END
480 :
490 :
500 REM Cannot calculate time
510 PRINT:PRINT:PRINT
520 PRINT"Repayment period cannot be calculated"
530 PRINT"on the information entered."
540 GOTO 430
```

P19   Depreciation

This program may be used to calculate the depreciation in the value of an article arising from normal use through time.

The program shows the effect of two common methods of calculating this depreciation.

1. The straight line method

   Under this method a fixed amount (a percentage of the initial value) is written off annually. The resultant graph shows a linear relationship between value and year. If, for example, the initial value was 8000 pounds, and 25% of this original value was written off each year, then we have:

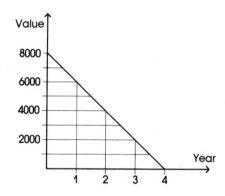

2. The diminishing balance method

Under this method a percentage of the residual value at the beginning of each year is written down at the end of that year. This gives a curve like:

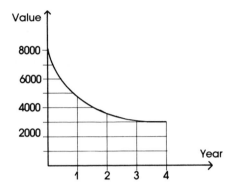

The program presents the two depreciation methods in the form of a table showing the amount to be written off over a period of years.

COMMANDS

Key in the program and RUN.
Follow the instructions.
Enter amounts as numbers only. This program works with any currency.

```
10 REM Depreciation
20 PAPER 0:INK 0,1
30 PEN 1:INK 1,24
40 BORDER 1
50 MODE 1
60 LOCATE 7,2
70 PRINT"DEPRECIATION CALCULATIONS"
80 PRINT TAB(7)"*************************"
90 LOCATE 1,5
```

```
100 PRINT"There are two  common  methods used to"
110 PRINT"calculate the depreciation of the value"
120 PRINT"of an asset over a given period.  These"
130 PRINT"are:"
140 LOCATE 7,11
150 PRINT"1. The straight line method;"
160 LOCATE 7,13
170 PRINT"2. The diminishing balance method."
180 LOCATE 1,18
190 PRINT"This program shows depreciation over a"
200 PRINT"fixed period using both metods.
210 LOCATE 7,23
220 PRINT"PRESS ANY KEY TO CONTINUE"
230 WHILE LEN(a$)=0:a$=INKEY$:WEND
240 :
250 CLS
260 IV=-1
270 WHILE IV<0
280 :   INPUT"Value of asset on acquisition";IV
290 WEND
300 :
310 A=-1
320 PRINT:PRINT
330 WHILE A<0
340 :   PRINT"If you wrote off a fixed amount each"
350 :   INPUT"year how much would it be";A
360 WEND
370 :
380 PR=-1
390 PRINT:PRINT
400 WHILE PR<0
410 :   PRINT"If you wrote off a percentage each"
420 :   INPUT"year, what would it be";PR
430 WEND
440 :
450 PRINT:PRINT
460 WHILE YR%<1 OR YR%>20
470 :   INPUT"Number of years to be presented";YR%
480 WEND
490 :
500 CLS
510 ZONE 13
520 PRINT"Year","Str. line","Dim. bal."
530 PRINT,"value","value"
540 PRINT
550 :
560 VA=IV
570 FOR n=1 TO YR%
580 :   VL=IV-A*n
590 :   IF VL<0 THEN VL=0
600 :   VA=VA*(100-PR)/100
610 :   IF VA<0 THEN VA=0
620 PRINT USING"###";n;
630 PRINT TAB(9) USING"##########.##";VL;VA
640 NEXT
650 :
660 WHILE LEN(b$)=0:b$=INKEY$:WEND
```

```
670 CLS
680 END
690 REM Any key ends program
```

Year	Str. line value	Dim. bal. value
1	850.00	700.00
2	700.00	490.00
3	550.00	343.00
4	400.00	240.10
5	250.00	168.07
6	100.00	117.65
7	0.00	82.35
8	0.00	57.65
9	0.00	40.35
10	0.00	28.25

P20   Cost of Sales Calculations

This program uses three different methods of calculating the
cost of sales, and uses the results of these calculations to
produce a report on Gross Profit

The methods are:

            1. First-In-First-Out
            2. Last-In-First-Out
            3. The method of Weighted Average

COMMANDS

Key in the program and RUN.
Follow the instructions.


```
10 REM Cost of sales calculation
20 PAPER 0:INK 0,1
30 PEN 1:INK 1,24
40 BORDER 1
50 MODE 1
60 :
70 PRINT TAB(7)"--------------------------"
80 PRINT TAB(7)"COST OF SALES CALCULATIONS"
90 PRINT TAB(7)"--------------------------"
100 PRINT:PRINT
110 PRINT"This program computes the cost of sales"
120 PRINT"using three different methods:"
130 PRINT
140 PRINT TAB(3)"first in first out,"
150 PRINT TAB(3)"last in first out,"
160 PRINT TAB(3)"weighted average."
170 PRINT:PRINT
180 PRINT"The results  of these  calculations are"
190 PRINT"then used to  produce a report on gross"
200 PRINT"profit."
210 PRINT:PRINT
220 WHILE pur%<=0
230 :   INPUT "Number of purchases made";pur%
240 WEND
250 :
260 DIM vol(pur%-1),pri(pur%-1)
270 FOR n=0 TO pur%-1
280 :   CLS
290 :   PRINT TAB(10)"PURCHASE NUMBER";n+1
300 :   PRINT:PRINT:PRINT
310 :   INPUT "Volume of purchase";vol(n)
320 :   PRINT
330 :   INPUT "Unit price of purchase";pri(n)
```

```
340 :   tp=tp+vol(n)
350 NEXT
360 :
370 CLS
380 WHILE sales%<=0
390 :   INPUT "Number of sales made";sales%
400 WEND
410 :
420 FOR n=0 TO sales%-1
430 :   CLS
440 :   PRINT TAB(13)"SALE NUMBER";n+1
450 :   PRINT:PRINT:PRINT
460 :   INPUT "Volume of sale";svol
470 :   PRINT
480 :   INPUT "Unit price of sale";spri
490 :   tt=tt+svol
500 :   rv=rv+svol*spri
510 NEXT
520 :
530 CLS
540 IF tt>tp THEN PRINT TAB(16)"OVERSOLD":GOSUB 1040:END
550 :
560 REM First in first out
570 t=tt
580 WHILE t>0
590 :   IF t>vol(ff) THEN t=t-vol(ff):c=c+vol(ff)*pri(ff)
600 :   IF t<=vol(ff) THEN c=c+t*pri(ff):t=0
610 :   ff=ff+1
620 WEND
630 :
640 PRINT"Using first in first out:"
650 GOSUB 940
660 :
670 REM Last in first out
680 t=tt:c=0:n=pur%-1
690 WHILE t>0
700 :   IF t>vol(n) THEN t=t-vol(n):c=c+vol(n)*pri(n)
710 :   IF t<=vol(n) THEN c=c+t*pri(n):t=0
720 :   n=n-1
730 WEND
740 :
750 PRINT"Using last in first out:"
760 GOSUB 940
770 :
780 REM Weighted average
790 FOR wt=0 TO pur%-1
800 :   pp=pp+vol(wt)*pri(wt)
810 NEXT
820 av=pp/tp
830 c=tt*av
840 :
850 PRINT"Using weighted average:"
860 GOSUB 940
870 GOSUB 1040
880 END
890 :
900 :
```

```
910 :
920 :
930 REM Print results
940 PRINT
950 PRINT"Revenue         =";USING "########.##";rv
960 PRINT"Cost of sales =";USING "########.##";c
970 PRINT"Gross profit  =";USING "########.##";rv-c
980 PRINT"-------------------------"
990 PRINT
1000 RETURN
1010 :
1020 :
1030 REM Any key to end
1040 PRINT
1050 PRINT"Press any key to end program."
1060 a$=INKEY$:IF LEN(a$)=0 THEN 1060
1070 CLS
1080 RETURN
```

P21 Four Weekly Moving Average

When attempting to measure trends in sales data it can be useful to plot the sales data along with a continually updated average of the last four weeks' sales.

This program performs such a task, with the sales data held in the form of data statements. Note that the data are terminated by an imaginary negative sale.

COMMANDS

Key in the program and RUN.
Follow instructions.


```
10 REM Four weekly moving average
20 PAPER 0:INK 0,0
30 PEN 1:INK 1,24
40 BORDER 0
50 MODE 1
60 :
70 PRINT TAB(7)"-------------------------"
80 PRINT TAB(7)"FOUR WEEKLY MOVING AVERAGE"
90 PRINT TAB(7)"-------------------------"
100 PRINT:PRINT
110 PRINT"This program  can be used to  assist in"
120 PRINT"the forecasting of sales  figures based"
130 PRINT"on a four week moving average."
140 PRINT:PRINT
150 PRINT"Note  that this  program does  not take"
160 PRINT"account of seasonal variations."
170 PRINT:PRINT
180 PRINT"Data are held in DATA statements. Up to"
190 PRINT"52 weeks can be handled."
200 PRINT:PRINT
210 PRINT"If necessary,  stop the program  to add"
220 PRINT"to or change the data."
230 :
240 DIM sa(53),ma(50)
250 REM Scale the data
260 WHILE fs>=0
270 :   READ sa(nm)
280 :   IF mx<sa(nm) THEN mx=sa(nm)
290 :   fs=sa(nm)
300 :   nm=nm+1
310 WEND
320 :
330 REM Calculate averages
340 FOR k=3 TO nm-2
350 :   ma(k-3)=(sa(k)+sa(k-1)+sa(k-2)+sa(k-3))/4
360 NEXT
```

```
370 :
380 PRINT:PRINT:PRINT
390 PRINT"Press any key to continue."
400 a$=INKEY$:IF LEN(a$)=0 THEN 400
410 :
420 MODE 2
430 REM Draw axes
440 PLOT 0,35
450 DRAWR 640,0
460 PLOT 50,0
470 DRAWR 0,400
480 :
490 FOR n=1 TO 6
500 :   LOCATE 5+11*n,24
510 :   PRINT 2*n;
520 NEXT
530 LOCATE 38,25
540 PRINT"Week number";
550 LOCATE 15,2
560 PRINT"Weekly sales - 1986"
570 :
580 vert=mx/25
590 FOR n=0 TO 4
600 :   LOCATE 1,23-n*5
610 :   PRINT INT((2+n*5)*vert)
620 NEXT
630 :
640 REM Draw sales
650 scale=400/mx
660 PLOT 50,sa(0)*scale
670 FOR n=1 TO nm-2
680 :   DRAW 50+11*n,sa(n)*scale
690 NEXT
700 :
710 REM Draw averages
720 PLOT 83,ma(0)*scale
730 FOR n=1 TO nm-5
740 :   DRAW 83+11*n,ma(n)*scale
750 NEXT
760 :
770 a$=INKEY$:IF LEN(a$)=0 THEN 770
780 REM Any key ends program
790 MODE 1
800 END
810 :
820 :
830 DATA 112,224,115,212,118,215,113,214,115,216,112
840 DATA 223,126,224,125,265,145,293,116,216,193,293
850 DATA 187,315,220,354,232,367,198,354,267,365,287
860 DATA 398,254,254,176,234,144,201,101,350,190,483
870 DATA 190,190
880 DATA -9
```

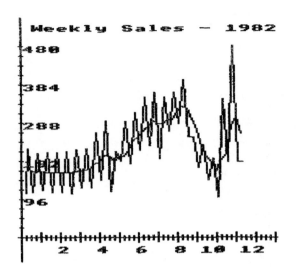

P22 Vat Calculator

This program calculates the Value Added Tax on an item and tells you both the tax and the total cost.

The results of the calculation are rounded to the nearest penny.

COMMANDS

Key in the program and RUN.
Enter data as required.

```
10 REM VAT Calculator
20 PAPER 0:INK 0,1
30 PEN 1:INK 1,24
40 BORDER 1
50 MODE 1
60 :
70 PRINT TAB(12)"--------------"
80 PRINT TAB(12)"VAT CALCULATOR"
90 PRINT TAB(12)"--------------"
100 PRINT:PRINT
110 PRINT"This program can be used to help you"
120 PRINT"make up your VAT returns."
130 LOCATE 1,14
140 PRINT"Current rate of VAT is 15%."
150 PRINT
160 INPUT"Do you wish to change this (y/n)";y$
170 vat=0.15
180 IF LEFT$(y$,1)="y" OR LEFT$(y$,1)="Y" THEN GOSUB 450
190 :
200 WHILE f=0
210 :   f=1
220 :   cost=-1
230 :   WHILE cost<0
240 :     CLS
250 :     INPUT"Cost of item";cost
260 :   WEND
270 :   LOCATE 1,7
280 :   PRINT"Cost of item =";
290 :   PRINT USING "##########.##";cost
300 :   LOCATE 1,10
310 :   PRINT"VAT          =";
320 :   PRINT USING "##########.##";cost*vat
330 :   LOCATE 1,13
340 :   PRINT"Total cost   =";
350 :   PRINT USING "##########.##";cost*(1+vat)
360 :   LOCATE 1,18
370 :   INPUT"Another item (y/n)";y$
380 :   IF LEFT$(y$,1)="y" OR LEFT$(y$,1)="Y" THEN f=0
390 WEND
```

```
400 CLS
410 END
420 :
430 :
440 REM VAT change subroutine
450 WHILE rate<=0
460 :    LOCATE 23,20
470 :    PRINT SPACE$(12)
480 :    LOCATE 1,20
490 :    INPUT"What is new rate (%)";rate
500 WEND
510 vat=rate/100
520 RETURN
```

P23 True Rate of Interest

This program uses a simplistic approach to calculating the true rate of interest on a loan. It is assumed that repayments are on a monthly basis.

To calculate the true rate of interest we compute the amount of pound-months that have been borrowed. (One pound-month is equivalent to borrowing one pound for one month, or fifty pence for two months.) We now calculate as a percentage the ratio of the total interest paid to the total number of pound-months. We then multiply this number by twelve.

As no monetary units are entered, this program is not limited to pounds and will work for any currency.

COMMANDS

Key in the program and RUN.
Follow the instructions.

```
10 REM True rate of interest
20 PAPER 0:INK 0,1
30 PEN 1:INK 1,24
40 BORDER 1
50 MODE 1
60 :
70 PRINT TAB(9)"---------------------"
80 PRINT TAB(9)"TRUE RATE OF INTEREST"
90 PRINT TAB(9)"---------------------"
100 PRINT:PRINT
110 PRINT"This program  computes the true rate of"
120 PRINT"interest  for a  loan transaction.  The"
130 PRINT"program  requires the amount  borrowed,"
140 PRINT"the annual interest rate and the number"
150 PRINT"of months over which the loan is taken."
160 PRINT:PRINT
170 INPUT"Amount  borrowed";amt
180 PRINT
190 INPUT"Annual  rate (%)";rate
200 PRINT
210 INPUT"Number of months";num
220 PRINT:PRINT
230 interest=amt*rate*num/1200
240 payback=(amt+interest)/num
250 :
260 REM Compound interest monthly
270 FOR month=1 TO num
280 :  borrowed=borrowed+(amt-payback*(month-1))
290 NEXT
300 :
310 true=1200*interest/borrowed
```

```
320 PRINT"True rate of interest is";
330 PRINT USING "####.##";true;
340 PRINT"%"
350 PRINT:PRINT
360 INPUT"Another run (y/n)";y$
370 IF LEFT$(y$,1)="y" OR LEFT$(y$,1)="Y" THEN RUN
380 CLS
390 END
```

Stock Control System

The next five programs form a rudimentary stock control system.

The first program lets you set up the stock file initially. In its present form it allows only ten different types of stock item. We are sure the reader will be able to amend the program to increase this number if necessary.

The next program is used to record all transactions, both additions to and withdrawals from stock. At present the program does not verify the data as it is entered. This would be a useful extension.

The third program updates the stock file with the information held in the transaction file. This is a fairly complicated program, which we have tried to make self explanatory by the use of PRINT and REM statements. This program also produces a list of items to be reordered.

The fourth program allows the full stock file to be printed out. This could be done after the stock file has been created or after it has been updated.

The final program allows the transaction file to be printed out, hence providing a hard copy of the day's transactions.

The full stock control system is:

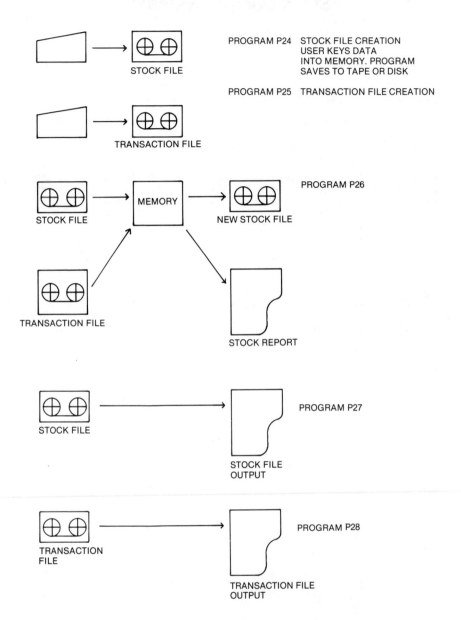

PROGRAM P24   STOCK FILE CREATION
USER KEYS DATA
INTO MEMORY. PROGRAM
SAVES TO TAPE OR DISK

PROGRAM P25   TRANSACTION FILE CREATION

STOCK FILE

TRANSACTION FILE

PROGRAM P26

STOCK FILE   MEMORY   NEW STOCK FILE

TRANSACTION FILE

STOCK REPORT

PROGRAM P27

STOCK FILE

STOCK FILE
OUTPUT

PROGRAM P28

TRANSACTION
FILE

TRANSACTION FILE
OUTPUT

P24 Stock File Creation

This program creates the stock file.

COMMANDS

Key in the program and RUN.
Have a blank tape or formatted disk ready.


```
10 REM Stock file creation
20 MODE 1
30 PAPER 0:INK 0,1
40 PEN 1:INK 1,24
50 BORDER 1
60 CLS
70 :
80 PRINT TAB(10)"-------------------"
90 PRINT TAB(10)"STOCK FILE CREATION"
100 PRINT TAB(10)"-------------------"
110 PRINT:PRINT
120 PRINT"This program  sets up a  stock  file of"
130 PRINT"up to ten items  on tape  or disk.  The"
140 PRINT"structure of each stock line is:"
150 PRINT
160 PRINT TAB(5)"Stock number (1 to 10)
170 PRINT TAB(5)"Description"
180 PRINT TAB(5)"Number in stock"
190 PRINT TAB(5)"Reorder level"
200 PRINT TAB(5)"Reorder quantity."
210 PRINT
220 PRINT"Please enter data as prompted.
230 PRINT"Enter eof as description to end entries."
240 PRINT
250 PRINT"Insert  the  storage  medium  (tape  or"
260 PRINT"disk) on which your stock file is to be"
270 PRINT"stored."
280 PRINT
290 PRINT"Press any key when ready."
300 a$=INKEY$:IF LEN(a$)=0 THEN 300
310 :
320 DIM des$(9)
330 DIM num(2,9)
340 WHILE items=0
350 :    IF d$="eof" AND stk=1 THEN stk=0
360 :    REM Zero length stock file unacceptable
370 :    CLS
380 :    PRINT TAB(13)"STOCK NUMBER";stk+1
390 :    PRINT:PRINT
400 :    INPUT"Description (eof to end)";des$(stk)
410 :    d$=LOWER$(des$(stk))
420 :    IF d$="eof" THEN items=stk ELSE GOSUB 680
430 :    stk=stk+1
```

```
440 :   IF stk=10 THEN items=10
450 WEND
460 :
470 REM Store stock file
480 CLS
490 OPENOUT "stock"
500 PRINT #9,items
510 r$=CHR$(13)
520 FOR n=1 TO items
530 :   k=n-1
540 :   PRINT #9,des$(k);r$;num(0,k);r$;num(1,k);r$;num(2,k)
550 NEXT
560 CLOSEOUT
570 PRINT:PRINT
580 PRINT"Eject your  storage  medium  and  label"
590 PRINT"with 'stock' and today's date."
600 PRINT:PRINT
610 PRINT"Press any key to end program."
620 a$=INKEY$:IF LEN(a$)=0 THEN 620
630 CLS
640 END
650 :
660 :
670 REM Get item details
680 PRINT
690 INPUT "Number in stock";num(0,stk)
700 PRINT
710 INPUT "Reorder level";num(1,stk)
720 PRINT
730 INPUT "Reorder quantity";num(2,stk)
740 RETURN
```

P25   Transaction File Creation

This program allows you to record up to 100 transactions.

COMMANDS

Key in the program and RUN.
Have a blank tape or formatted disk ready.


```
10 REM Transaction file creation
20 MODE 1
30 PAPER 0:INK 0,1
40 PEN 1:INK 1,24
50 BORDER 1
60 CLS
70 :
80 PRINT TAB(7)"-------------------------"
90 PRINT TAB(7)"TRANSACTION FILE CREATION"
100 PRINT TAB(7)"-------------------------"
110 PRINT:PRINT
120 PRINT"This program  allows up to  one hundred"
130 PRINT"transactions  to be recorded  against a"
140 PRINT"stock file."
150 PRINT:PRINT
160 PRINT"The structure  of the  transaction file"
170 PRINT"is:"
180 PRINT
190 PRINT TAB(6)"stock number"
200 PRINT TAB(6)"code   1 - withdrawal"
210 PRINT TAB(12)"2 - addition"
220 PRINT
230 PRINT"Please enter details when  prompted.  A"
240 PRINT"negative stock number terminates entry."
250 PRINT:PRINT
260 PRINT"Insert   the  storage  medium  (tape  or"
270 PRINT"disk) on which your  stock file is held"
280 PRINT"Press any key when ready."
290 a$=INKEY$:IF LEN(a$)=0 THEN 290
300 :
310 CLS
320 OPENIN "stock"
330 INPUT #9,items
340 DIM des$(items-1)
350 FOR n=1 TO items
360 :   INPUT #9,des$(n-1),a,b,c
370 NEXT
380 CLOSEIN
390 :
400 PRINT:PRINT
410 PRINT"Eject the stock file tape or disk."
420 PRINT
```

```
430 PRINT"Insert  the  storage  medium  (tape  or"
440 PRINT"disk) on which your transaction file is"
450 PRINT"to be stored. Press any key when ready."
460 a$=INKEY$:IF LEN(a$)=0 THEN 460
470 :
480 DIM stk%(99)
490 DIM trc%(99)
500 DIM quan(99)
510 WHILE exit=0
520 :  CLS
530 :  PRINT"Enter a negative stock number to end."
540 :  PRINT:PRINT:PRINT
550 :  WHILE stk%(trans)>items OR stk%(trans)<1
560 :    PRINT"Stock number ( 1 to";items;")";
570 :    INPUT stk%(trans)
580 :    a=stk%(trans)
590 :    IF a<0 THEN exit=1:stk%(trans)=1 ELSE GOSUB 870
600 :  WEND
610 :  IF exit=0 THEN trans=trans+1
620 :  IF trans=100 THEN exit=1
630 WEND
640 :
650 CLS
660 IF trans=0 THEN PRINT"No transactions recorded":END
670 OPENOUT "tranfile"
680 r$=CHR$(13)
690 PRINT #9,items;r$;trans
700 FOR n=1 TO items:PRINT #9,des$(n-1):NEXT
710 FOR n=1 TO trans
720 :  PRINT #9,stk%(n-1);r$;trc%(n-1);r$;quan(n-1)
730 NEXT
740 CLOSEOUT
750 PRINT:PRINT
760 PRINT"Stop datacorder and rewind to the start"
770 PRINT"of the file.  Eject cassette  and label"
780 PRINT"with 'tranfile' and today's date."
790 PRINT:PRINT
800 PRINT"Press any key to end program."
810 a$=INKEY$:IF LEN(a$)=0 THEN 810
820 CLS
830 END
840 :
850 :
860 REM Get code and quantity
870 IF a>items OR a<1 THEN RETURN
880 PRINT
890 PRINT"Description - ";des$(a-1)
900 PRINT
910 WHILE trc%(trans)<1 OR trc%(trans)>2
920 :  PRINT"Transaction code - "
930 :  INPUT "(1 -  withdrawal: 2 - addition)";trc%(trans)
940 WEND
950 PRINT
960 INPUT"Quantity";quan(trans)
970 RETURN
```

P26 Stock File Update and Report

This program updates the stock file and produces a list of items to be ordered. The program requires a printer.

COMMANDS

Key in the program and RUN.
Have your stock file, transaction file and a blank tape or blank formatted disk handy.


```
10 REM Stock file update and report
20 MODE 1
30 PAPER 0:INK 0,1
40 PEN 1:INK 1,24
50 BORDER 1
60 CLS
70 :
80 PRINT TAB(11)"------------------"
90 PRINT TAB(11)"STOCK FILE UPDATE"
100 PRINT TAB(14)"AND REPORT"
110 PRINT TAB(11)"------------------"
120 PRINT:PRINT
130 PRINT"This program updates  a stock file with"
140 PRINT"the contents  of a transaction file.  A"
150 PRINT"list of items to  be reordered  is then"
160 PRINT"printed out."
170 PRINT:PRINT
180 PRINT"Insert the tape or disk  on which  your"
190 PRINT"current stock file is held."
200 PRINT:PRINT
210 GOSUB 1080
220 :
230 CLS
240 OPENIN "stock"
250 INPUT #9,items
260 DIM des$(items-1)
270 DIM num(2,items-1)
280 FOR n=0 TO items-1
290 :  INPUT #9,des$(n),num(0,n),num(1,n),num(2,n)
300 NEXT
310 CLOSEIN
320 :
330 PRINT:PRINT
340 PRINT"Eject the stock file tape or disk."
350 PRINT
360 PRINT"Insert  the  transaction  file  tape or"
370 PRINT"disk."
380 PRINT:PRINT
390 GOSUB 1080
400 PRINT
410 :
```

```
420 OPENIN "tranfile"
430 INPUT #9,it
440 IF it<>items THEN PRINT"Wrong file":CLOSEIN:END
450 INPUT #9,trans
460 DIM trc(2,trans-1)
470 FOR n=0 TO items-1
480 :  INPUT #9,d$
490 :  IF d$<>des$(n) THEN wrong=1:n=items-1
500 NEXT
510 IF wrong=1 THEN PRINT"Wrong file":CLOSEIN:END
520 FOR n=0 TO trans-1
530 :  INPUT #9,trc(0,n),trc(1,n),trc(2,n)
540 NEXT
550 CLOSEIN
560 :
570 PRINT:PRINT
580 PRINT"Eject the transaction file tape or disk."
590 PRINT"Insert the  tape or  disk on  which you"
600 PRINT"wish to save the updated stock file."
610 PRINT:PRINT
620 GOSUB 1080
630 :
640 CLS
650 PRINT"File being updated."
660 PRINT:PRINT
670 FOR n=0 TO trans-1
680 :  sn=trc(0,n)-1
690 :  IF trc(1,n)=1 THEN num(0,sn)=num(0,sn)-trc(2,n)
700 :  IF trc(1,n)=2 THEN num(0,sn)=num(0,sn)+trc(2,n)
710 :  PRINT".";
720 NEXT
730 PRINT:PRINT
740 PRINT"Updating complete. New stock file being"
750 PRINT"saved."
760 PRINT:PRINT
770 :
780 OPENOUT "stock"
790 r$=CHR$(13)
800 PRINT #9,items
810 FOR n=0 TO items-1
820 :  PRINT #9,des$(n);r$;num(0,n);r$;num(1,n);r$;num(2,n)
830 NEXT
840 CLOSEOUT
850 :
860 CLS
870 PRINT"Eject tape or disk.  Label with 'stock'"
880 PRINT"and today's date."
890 PRINT:PRINT
900 PRINT"Ensure your printer  is switched  on and"
910 PRINT"loaded with paper."
920 PRINT:PRINT
930 GOSUB 1080
940 :
950 PRINT #8,"Items to be reordered:"
960 PRINT #8,
970 PRINT #8,
980 FOR n=0 TO items-1
```

```
990 :    IF num(0,n)<=num(1,n) THEN GOSUB 1140
1000 NEXT
1010 PRINT #8,"Negative numbers mean customers waiting"
1020 PRINT #8,"for goods."
1030 CLS
1040 END
1050 :
1060 :
1070 REM Any key
1080 PRINT"Press any key when ready."
1090 a$=INKEY$:IF LEN(a$)=0 THEN 1090
1100 RETURN
1110 :
1120 :
1130 REM Print details
1140 PRINT #8,"Stock number",,n+1
1150 PRINT #8,"Description",,CHR$(32);des$(n)
1160 PRINT #8,"Number in stock",num(0,n)
1170 PRINT #8,"Reorder level",num(1,n)
1180 PRINT #8,"Reorder quantity",num(2,n)
1190 PRINT #8,
1200 PRINT #8,
1210 RETURN
```

P27 Stock File Output

The program outputs a stock file, which has been saved on tape or disk, to a printer.

COMMANDS

Key in the program and RUN.
Have your stock file tape or disk handy.


```
10 REM Stock file output
20 MODE 1
30 PAPER 0:INK 0,1
40 PEN 1:INK 1,24
50 BORDER 1
60 CLS
70 :
80 PRINT TAB(11)"-----------------"
90 PRINT TAB(11)"STOCK FILE OUTPUT
100 PRINT TAB(11)"-----------------"
110 PRINT:PRINT
120 PRINT"This program  reads a  stock file  from"
130 PRINT"tape or disk and lists it to a printer."
140 PRINT:PRINT
150 PRINT"Insert the stock file tape or disk."
160 PRINT:PRINT
170 PRINT"Press any key when ready."
180 a$=INKEY$:IF LEN(a$)=0 THEN 180
190 :
200 PRINT
210 OPENIN "stock"
220 INPUT #9,items
230 DIM des$(items-1)
240 DIM num(2,items-1)
250 FOR n=0 TO items-1
260 :   INPUT #9,des$(n),num(0,n),num(1,n),num(2,n)
270 NEXT
280 CLOSEIN
290 :
300 CLS
310 PRINT"Eject tape or disk."
320 PRINT:PRINT
330 PRINT"Ensure printer is switched on and loaded"
340 PRINT"with paper."
350 PRINT:PRINT
360 PRINT"Press any key when ready."
370 a$=INKEY$:IF LEN(a$)=0 THEN 370
380 PRINT #8,"STOCK FILE"
390 PRINT #8,"----------"
400 PRINT #8,
410 PRINT #8,
420 FOR n=0 TO items-1
```

```
430 :   PRINT #8,"Stock number",,n+1
440 :   PRINT #8,"Description",,CHR$(32);des$(n)
450 :   PRINT #8,"Number in stock",num(0,n)
460 :   PRINT #8,"Reorder level",num(1,n)
470 :   PRINT #8,"Reorder quantity",num(2,n)
480 :   PRINT #8,
490 :   PRINT #8,
500 NEXT
510 PRINT #8,"Negative numbers mean customers waiting"
520 PRINT #8,"for goods."
530 CLS
540 END
```

P28 Transaction File Output

The program outputs a transaction file, which has been saved on tape or disk, to a printer.

COMMANDS

Key in the program and RUN.
Have your transaction file tape or disk handy.


```
10 REM Transaction file output
20 MODE 1
30 PAPER 0:INK 0,1
40 PEN 1:INK 1,24
50 BORDER 1
60 CLS
70 :
80 PRINT TAB(8)"----------------------"
90 PRINT TAB(8)"TRANSACTION FILE OUTPUT"
100 PRINT TAB(8)"----------------------"
110 PRINT:PRINT
120 PRINT"This program  reads  a transaction file"
130 PRINT"from tape or  disk and lists  it to the"
140 PRINT"printer."
150 PRINT
160 PRINT"This enables the user  to obtain a hard"
170 PRINT"copy of the day's transactions."
180 PRINT:PRINT
190 PRINT"Insert  the  tape or disk  on which the"
200 PRINT"transaction file is stored."
210 PRINT:PRINT
220 PRINT"Press any key when ready."
230 a$=INKEY$:IF LEN(a$)=0 THEN 230
240 :
250 PRINT
260 OPENIN "tranfile"
270 INPUT #9,items,trans
280 DIM des$(items-1)
290 DIM num(2,trans-1)
300 FOR n=0 TO items-1:INPUT #9,des$(n):NEXT
310 FOR n=0 TO trans-1
320 :  INPUT #9,num(0,n),num(1,n),num(2,n)
330 NEXT
340 CLOSEIN
350 :
360 CLS
370 PRINT"Eject tape or disk."
380 PRINT:PRINT
390 PRINT"Ensure printer is switched on and loaded"
400 PRINT"with paper."
410 PRINT:PRINT
420 PRINT"Press any key when ready."
```

```
430 a$=INKEY$:IF LEN(a$)=0 THEN 430
440 PRINT #8,"TRANSACTION FILE"
450 PRINT #8,"----------------"
460 PRINT #8,
470 PRINT #8,
480 FOR n=0 TO trans-1
490 sn=num(0,n)
500 :   PRINT #8,"Stock number",,sn
510 :   PRINT #8,"Description",,CHR$(32);des$(sn-1)
520 IF num(1,n)=1 THEN t$="withdrawal" ELSE t$="addition"
530 :   PRINT #8,"Transaction code",num(1,n);"- ";t$
540 :   PRINT #8,"Quantity",,num(2,n)
550 :   PRINT #8,
560 :   PRINT #8,
570 NEXT
580 CLS
590 END
```

P29   Mailing List Creation

This program allows you to create a mailing list of up to fifty names and addresses and to save this information on tape or disk.

It could be extended to take more names and addresses.

COMMANDS

Key in the program and RUN.
Ensure you have a blank tape or formatted disk handy.
Follow the instructions.

```
10 REM Mailing list creation
20 MODE 1
30 PAPER 0:INK 0,1
40 PEN 1:INK 1,24
50 BORDER 1
60 CLS
70 :
80 PRINT TAB(9)"--------------------"
90 PRINT TAB(9)"MAILING LIST CREATION"
100 PRINT TAB(9)"--------------------"
110 PRINT:PRINT
120 PRINT"This program allows  you to  type in up"
130 PRINT"to fifty names  and addresses and  save"
140 PRINT"these as a mailing list file."
150 PRINT
160 PRINT"Each address should  be limited to four"
170 PRINT"lines, including the post code."
180 PRINT
190 PRINT"Please enter data when prompted."
200 PRINT
210 PRINT"Press any key to continue."
220 a$=INKEY$:IF LEN(a$)=0 THEN 220
230 :
240 DIM nm$(49)
250 DIM ad$(49,3)
260 FOR n=0 TO 49
270 :   CLS
280 :   PRINT TAB(6)"Enter end as name to finish"
290 :   PRINT:PRINT
300 :   INPUT "Name";nm$(n)
310 :   fs=0
320 :   WHILE LOWER$(nm$(n))<>"end" AND fs=0
330 :     PRINT"Address:"
340 :     INPUT "Line 1";ad$(n,0)
350 :     INPUT "Line 2";ad$(n,1)
360 :     INPUT "Line 3";ad$(n,2)
```

```
370 :      INPUT "post code";ad$(n,3)
380 :        fs=1
390 :    WEND
400 :    IF LOWER$(nm$(n))="end" THEN n=49
410 NEXT
420 :
430 CLS
440 PRINT"Insert the  tape or disk  on  which you"
450 PRINT"wish to save your mailing list."
460 PRINT:PRINT
470 INPUT "What is the name of the file";nam$
480 IF LEN(nam$)>8 THEN nam$=LEFT$(nam$,8)
490 PRINT:PRINT
500 :
510 OPENOUT nam$
520 FOR n=0 TO 49
530 :    fs=0
540 :    WHILE LOWER$(nm$(n))<>"end" AND fs=0
550 :      PRINT #9,nm$(n)
560 :      FOR k=0 TO 3:PRINT #9,ad$(n,k):NEXT
570 :        fs=1
580 :    WEND
590 :    IF LOWER$(nm$(n))="end" THEN n=49
600 NEXT
610 CLOSEOUT
620 CLS
630 END
```

P30 Mailing List Maintenance

This program lets you amend a previously created mailing list and save the new list on tape or disk.

The program could be extended to deal with more than fifty names and addresses.

COMMANDS

Key in the program and RUN.
Ensure you have your mailing list tape and a blank tape or formatted disk ready.

```
10 REM Mailing list maintenance
20 MODE 1
30 PAPER 0:INK 0,1
40 PEN 1:INK 1,24
50 BORDER 1
60 CLS
70 :
80 PRINT TAB(7)"-----------------------"
90 PRINT TAB(7)"MAILING LIST MAINTENANCE"
100 PRINT TAB(7)"-----------------------"
110 PRINT:PRINT
120 PRINT"This program allows you to add names to"
130 PRINT"and  delete names  from a  mailing list"
140 PRINT"which you  have previously  created and"
150 PRINT"saved to tape or disk."
160 PRINT:PRINT
170 PRINT"Insert the tape or disk containing your"
180 PRINT"mailing list file."
190 PRINT:PRINT
200 INPUT "What is the name of the file";nam$
210 IF LEN(nam$)>8 THEN nam$=LEFT$(nam$,8)
220 PRINT
230 :
240 DIM nm$(49)
250 DIM ad$(49,3)
260 OPENIN nam$
270 WHILE EOF=0
280 :  INPUT #9,nm$(n),ad$(n,0),ad$(n,1),ad$(n,2),ad$(n,3)
290 :  n=n+1
300 WEND
310 entries=n-1
320 :
330 sl=5
340 WHILE sl<>4
350 :  CLS
360 :  IF sl=5 THEN PRINT"Eject tape or disk."
370 :  PRINT:PRINT
380 :  PRINT"Select the operation required by"
390 :  PRINT"pressing:"
```

```
400 :   PRINT:PRINT
410 :   PRINT TAB(6)"Key 1 - Add addresses"
420 :   PRINT TAB(6)"Key 2 - Remove addresses"
430 :   PRINT TAB(6)"Key 3 - Save new mail list"
440 :   PRINT TAB(6)"Key 4 - End program
450 :   a$=""
460 :   WHILE a$<>"1" AND a$<>"2" AND a$<>"3" AND a$<>"4"
470 :     a$=INKEY$
480 :   WEND
490 :   sl=ASC(a$)-48
500 :   ON sl GOSUB 570,890,1360
510 WEND
520 CLS
530 END
540 :
550 :
560 REM Add to list
570 exit=0:any=2
580 WHILE exit=0 AND entries<49
590 :   CLS
600 :   PRINT TAB(8)"ENTERING NEW INFORMATION"
610 :   PRINT:PRINT:PRINT
620 :   PRINT"Enter end as name to finish."
630 :   PRINT:PRINT
640 :   INPUT "Name";nm$(entries+1)
650 :   fs=0
660 :   ar$=LOWER$(nm$(entries+1))
670 :   WHILE fs=0 AND ar$<>"end"
680 :     PRINT"Address:"
690 :     INPUT "line 1";ad$(entries+1,0)
700 :     INPUT "line 2";ad$(entries+1,1)
710 :     INPUT "line 3";ad$(entries+1,2)
720 :     INPUT "post code";ad$(entries+1,3)
730 :     entries=entries+1
740 :     fs=1
750 :     any=1
760 :   WEND
770 :   IF ar$="end" THEN exit=1
780 WEND
790 :
800 CLS
810 IF entries=49 THEN PRINT"Mailing list full."
820 PRINT
830 IF any=1 THEN PRINT"New information has been added."
840 ON any GOSUB 1580,1660
850 RETURN
860 :
870 :
880 REM Delete addresses
890 exit=0:any=2
900 WHILE exit=0
910 :   CLS
920 :   PRINT TAB(9)"DELETING INFORMATION"
930 :   PRINT:PRINT
940 :   PRINT"Please    enter    the    exact    name"
950 :   PRINT"corresponding to  the entry you wish to"
960 :   PRINT"delete.   If   there   are  two  addresses"
```

```
970 :    PRINT"corresponding to the same name, both of"
980 :    PRINT"these will be deleted."
990 :   PRINT:PRINT
1000 :   INPUT "Name";nam$
1010 :   r=50
1020 :   FOR k=0 TO entries
1030 :      IF nm$(k)=nam$ THEN r=k:k=enties:any=1
1040 :   NEXT
1050 :   PRINT:PRINT
1060 :   IF r=50 THEN PRINT"Name not found."
1070 :   fs=0
1080 :   IF r<50 AND entries=0 THEN exit=1:entries=-1:fs=1
1090 :   WHILE fs=0 AND r<50
1100 :      PRINT"Updating"
1110 :      PRINT
1120 :      FOR k=r TO entries-1
1130 :         nm$(k)=nm$(k+1)
1140 :         FOR j=0 TO 3:ad$(k,j)=ad$(k+1,j):NEXT
1150 :         PRINT".";
1160 :      NEXT
1170 :      entries=entries-1
1180 :      fs=1
1190 :   WEND
1200 :   PRINT:PRINT
1210 :   IF exit=0 THEN INPUT "Another deletion (y/n)";y$
1220 :   y$=LOWER$(LEFT$(y$,1))
1230 :   IF y$<>"y" THEN exit=1
1240 WEND
1250 :
1260 CLS
1270 IF entries=-1 THEN PRINT"Mailing list empty."
1280 PRINT:PRINT
1290 IF any=1 THEN PRINT"Entries have been deleted."
1300 IF entries=-1 THEN any=2
1310 ON any GOSUB 1580,1660
1320 RETURN
1330 :
1340 :
1350 REM Save new file
1360 CLS
1370 IF entries=-1 THEN PRINT"Empty file.":GOSUB 1660:RETURN
1380 PRINT"Insert  the  tape or disk  on which you"
1390 PRINT"wish to save the new mailing list."
1400 PRINT:PRINT
1410 INPUT "What is the name of the new list";nl$
1420 IF LEN (nl$)>8 THEN nl$=LEFT$(nl$,8)
1430 PRINT
1440 OPENOUT nl$
1450 FOR n=0 TO entries
1460 PRINT #9,nm$(n)
1470 :   FOR j=0 TO 3:PRINT #9,ad$(n,j):NEXT
1480 NEXT
1490 CLOSEOUT
1500 PRINT:PRINT
1510 PRINT"Eject tape or  disk and label  with the"
1520 PRINT"file name and today's date."
1530 GOSUB 1660
```

```
1540 RETURN
1550 :
1560 :
1570 REM Addition or removal complete
1580 PRINT:PRINT
1590 PRINT"Remember you still have to save the new"
1600 PRINT"list if you have finished updating it."
1610 GOSUB 1660
1620 RETURN
1630 :
1640 :
1650 REM Any key
1660 PRINT:PRINT
1670 PRINT"Press any key to return to main menu."
1680 k$=INKEY$:IF LEN(k$)=0 THEN 1680
1690 RETURN
```

P31 Mailing List Output

This program lets you print the names and addresses on a mailing list on to labels.

A useful additional feature would be a search facility which would allow you to specify that only names starting with (say) a particular letter would be printed out. Another useful feature would be the facility to display a telephone dialling code on the screen when a name is typed in.

COMMANDS

Key in the program and RUN.
Ensure you have your mailing list tape or disk ready.
If necessary, adjust the lines indicated by the REM statements in the code to get the optimum print positioning on your labels.

```
10 REM Mailing list output
20 PAPER 0:INK 0,1
30 PEN 1:INK 1,24
40 BORDER 1
50 MODE 1
60 :
70 PRINT TAB(10)"-------------------"
80 PRINT TAB(10)"MAILING LIST OUTPUT"
90 PRINT TAB(10)"-------------------"
100 PRINT:PRINT
110 PRINT"This program allows you to print labels"
120 PRINT"from the  data held  in a  mailing list"
130 PRINT"which you  have previously  created and"
140 PRINT"saved to tape or disk."
150 PRINT:PRINT
160 PRINT"Insert the tape or disk containing your"
170 PRINT"mailing list file."
180 PRINT:PRINT
190 INPUT "What is the name of the file";nam$
200 IF LEN(nam$)>8 THEN nam$=LEFT$(nam$,8)
210 PRINT
220 :
230 DIM nm$(49)
240 DIM ad$(49,3)
250 OPENIN nam$
260 WHILE EOF=0
270 :   INPUT #9,nm$(n),ad$(n,0),ad$(n,1),ad$(n,2),ad$(n,3)
280 :   n=n+1
290 WEND
300 entries=n-1
310 :
320 CLS
330 PRINT"Eject your tape or disk."
```

```
340 PRINT:PRINT
350 PRINT"Ensure that the blank labels are loaded"
360 PRINT"into  your  printer and  are  correctly"
370 PRINT"positioned."
380 PRINT:PRINT
390 PRINT"Press any key when ready."
400 a$=INKEY$:IF LEN(a$)=0 THEN 400
410 :
420 mar=10:REM adjust this line to position print on labels
430 FOR n=0 TO entries
440 :   PRINT #8,TAB(mar);nm$(n)
450 :   FOR j=0 TO 3
460 :     PRINT #8,TAB(mar);ad$(n,j)
470 :   NEXT
480 :   FOR k=0 TO 2:PRINT #8:NEXT
490 :   REM Adjust previous line to get correct spacing
500 :   REM between labels.
510 NEXT
520 CLS
530 END
```

P32 Monthly Accounts

In our households, one of the tasks which has to be done is the monthly budget. It seemed to us that this was an ideal use for the microcomputer.

Once the program is running, it prompts users to enter all their outgoings and income. The program ends with a report onto paper or screen of the monthly budget.

COMMANDS

Key in the program and RUN.
Follow the instructions.


```
10 REM Monthly accounts
20 PAPER 0:INK 0,24
30 PEN 1:INK 1,30
40 BORDER 24
50 MODE 1
60 :
70 PRINT TAB(12)"----------------"
80 PRINT TAB(12)"MONTHLY ACCOUNTS"
90 PRINT TAB(12)"----------------"
100 PRINT:PRINT
110 PRINT"This  program helps you to  budget your"
120 PRINT"monthly income and expenditure."
130 PRINT
140 PRINT"It prompts you to enter your  financial"
150 PRINT"dealings and  produces a balance sheet."
160 PRINT
170 PRINT"If you wish  to use  a printer,  please"
180 PRINT"ensure that this is connected, switched"
190 PRINT"on and loaded with paper.
200 PRINT
210 PRINT"Press any key when ready."
220 a$=INKEY$:IF LEN(a$)=0 THEN 220
230 :
240 CLS
250 PRINT TAB(11)"REGULAR OUTGOINGS"
260 PRINT
270 PRINT
280 INPUT "Mortgage repayment";mort
290 INPUT "Rates payment";rates
300 INPUT "Rent payment";rent
310 INPUT "Electricity";elec
320 INPUT "Gas";gas
330 :
340 REM Take in all credit repayments
350 c=1
360 PRINT
```

```
370 PRINT
380 PRINT TAB(9)"CREDIT CARD REPAYMENTS"
390 PRINT
400 WHILE c<>0
410 :   INPUT "Credit repayment (0 for last)";c
420 :   credit=credit+c
430 WEND
440 :
450 PRINT
460 PRINT
470 INPUT "Other regular payments (total)";other
480 PRINT
490 reg=mort+rates++rent+elec+gas+credit+other
500 :
510 REM Get other outgoings
520 CLS
530 PRINT TAB(8)"OTHER OUTGOINGS THIS MONTH"
540 PRINT
550 PRINT"Use  estimates  if  actual  amounts not"
560 PRINT"known."
570 PRINT
580 PRINT
590 INPUT "Bills outstanding (total)";oldbills
600 INPUT "Grocery bill";groc
610 INPUT "Butcher's bill";butch
620 INPUT "Travel costs";trav
630 INPUT "Entertainment allowance";entr
640 PRINT
650 PRINT
660 PRINT TAB(8)"OTHER BILLS DUE THIS MONTH"
670 PRINT
680 b=1
690 WHILE b<>0
700 :   INPUT "Amount of bill (0 to end)";b
710 :   otherbills=otherbills+b
720 WEND
730 :
740 monthbills=groc+butch+trav+entr+otherbills
750 totalout=reg+monthbills+oldbills
760 :
770 REM Get income
780 CLS
790 PRINT TAB(12)"MONTHLY INCOME"
800 PRINT
810 PRINT
820 INPUT "Enter your monthly income ",inc1
830 PRINT
840 INPUT "Enter spouse's monthly income ",inc2
850 PRINT
860 INPUT "Enter any other net income ",inc3
870 PRINT
880 PRINT
890 income=inc1+inc2+inc3
900 balance=income-totalout
910 :
920 PRINT"Select output device by pressing:"
930 PRINT
```

```
940 PRINT TAB(6)"Key 1 for screen"
950 PRINT TAB(6)"Key 2 for printer."
960 a$=INKEY$:IF a$<>"1" AND a$<>"2" THEN 960
970 IF a$="2" THEN cha=8
980 CLS
990 PRINT #cha,TAB(12)"MONTHLY BUDGET"
1000 PRINT #cha,TAB(12)"--------------"
1010 PRINT #cha
1020 PRINT #cha
1030 PRINT #cha,"COMMENT";SPC(14)"OUT";SPC(8)"IN"
1040 PRINT #cha,"-----------------------------------"
1050 PRINT #cha
1060 PRINT #cha,"Regular payments";SPC(3);
1070 PRINT #cha, USING "####.##";reg
1080 PRINT #cha
1090 PRINT #cha,"Bills this month"SPC(3);
1100 PRINT #cha, USING "####.##";monthbills
1110 PRINT #cha
1120 PRINT #cha,"Outstanding bills";SPC(2);
1130 PRINT #cha, USING "####.##";oldbills
1140 PRINT #cha
1150 PRINT #cha, TAB(20)"-------"
1160 PRINT #cha,"TOTAL OUT";SPC(10);
1170 PRINT #cha, USING "####.##";totalout
1180 PRINT #cha
1190 PRINT #cha, TAB(31)"-------"
1200 PRINT #cha,"TOTAL INCOME";SPC(18);
1210 PRINT #cha, USING "####.##";income
1220 PRINT #cha
1230 IF balance<0 THEN PRINT #cha,"DEBIT BALANCE";SPC(17)
1240 IF balance>=0 THEN PRINT #cha,"CREDIT BALANCE";SPC(5);
1250 PRINT #cha, USING "####.##";ABS(balance)
1260 IF balance<0 THEN PRINT #cha, TAB(31)"======="
1270 IF balance>=0 THEN PRINT #cha, TAB(20)"======="
1280 :
1290 PRINT #cha
1300 PRINT"Press any key to end program."
1310 a$=INKEY$:IF LEN(a$)=0 THEN 1310
1320 CLS
1330 END
```

P33 Conversion

This is a general purpose conversion utility, which we have implemented with eighteen different conversion factors. It is fairly straightforward to choose other units to be converted by changing the data statements at the end of the program.

Eighteen conversion factors were chosen to make the main menu fit the screen.

Once the conversion has been chosen, you have to decide which way the conversion has to proceed. For example, centimetres to inches or inches to centimetres.

COMMANDS

Key in the program and RUN.
Select from menu.


```
10 REM Conversion
20 PAPER 0:INK 0,26
30 PEN 1:INK 1,5
40 BORDER 26
50 MODE 1
60 :
70 PRINT TAB(15)"=========="
80 PRINT TAB(15)"CONVERSION"
90 PRINT TAB(15)"=========="
100 PRINT:PRINT
110 PRINT"This   program   is   a   general   purpose"
120 PRINT"conversion utility. The conversion data"
130 PRINT"are held within the program."
140 PRINT:PRINT
150 PRINT"Press any key to continue."
160 a$=INKEY$:IF LEN(a$)=0 THEN 160
170 :
180 DIM it$(17,1),fa(17)
190 FOR n=0 TO 17
200 :  READ it$(n,0),it$(n,1)
210 NEXT
220 FOR n=0 TO 17
230 :  READ fa(n)
240 NEXT
250 :
260 y$="y"
270 WHILE LOWER$(LEFT$(y$,1))="y"
280 :  CLS
290 :  PRINT TAB(10)"CONVERSIONS AVAILABLE"
300 :  PRINT
310 :  FOR n=0 TO 17
320 :  PRINT USING "##";n+1;
330 :    PRINT SPC(4);it$(n,0);" to ";it$(n,1)
```

```
340 :   NEXT
350 :   PRINT
360 :   PRINT"Choose item by entering the appropriate"
370 :   PRINT"number."
380 :   INPUT "What is your choice";ch%
390 :   IF ch%<1 OR ch%>18 THEN 280
400 :
410 :   CLS
420 :   c=ch%-1
430 :   PRINT TAB(10)"OPTIONS AVAILABLE"
440 :   PRINT:PRINT
450 :   PRINT "1. ";it$(c,0);" to ";it$(c,1)
460 :   PRINT "2. ";it$(c,1);" to ";it$(c,0)
470 :   PRINT:PRINT
480 :   PRINT"Select by pressing Key 1 or Key 2"
490 :   a$=INKEY$:IF a$<>"1" AND a$<>"2" THEN 490
500 :   ON VAL(a$) GOSUB 650,720
510 :   PRINT:PRINT
520 :   PRINT"Enter value of ";t1$;
530 :   INPUT aa
540 :   PRINT:PRINT
550 :   PRINT aa;t1$;" =";fact*aa;t2$
560 :   PRINT:PRINT
570 :   INPUT "Another conversion (y/n)";y$
580 WEND
590 :
600 CLS
610 END
620 :
630 :
640 REM First option
650 fact=fa(c)
660 t1$=it$(c,0)
670 t2$=it$(c,1)
680 RETURN
690 :
700 :
710 REM Second option
720 fact=1/fa(c)
730 t1$=it$(c,1)
740 t2$=it$(c,0)
750 RETURN
760 :
770 :
780 REM Items data
790 DATA inches,cm,feet,metres,yards,metres,miles
800 DATA kilometres,teaspoons,cc,tablespoons,cc,cups
810 DATA litres,pints,litres,quarts,litres,gallons
820 DATA litres,ounces,grams,pounds,kilograms,tons
830 DATA kilograms,miles/hour,metres/second
840 DATA square yards,square metres,years,seconds
850 DATA atmospheres,cm Hg,acres,hectares
860 :
870 :
880 REM Conversion data
890 DATA 2.54,.3048,.9144,1.609,4.929,14.788
900 DATA .2366,.5683,1.1365,4.546,28.3495
```

```
910 DATA .4536,907.2,.447,.8631,3.16E7
920 DATA 76,.4047
```

P34   Birthday List

This program uses one of the SORT routines developed elsewhere in the book, the so-called Bubble Sort.

The Birthday List program is used to store all those birthdays that you have to remember. The program sorts the birthdays into date order, and then prints out all bithdays left in the current year. All birthdays are stored in data statements.

COMMANDS

Key in the program and RUN.
Follow instructions.
When you can folllow the operation of the program, amend the data statements.


```
10 REM Birthday list
20 PAPER 0:INK 0,23
30 PEN 1:INK 1,30
40 BORDER 23
50 MODE 1
60 :
70 PRINT TAB(14)">>>>>>>>>>>>>"
80 PRINT TAB(14)"BIRTHDAY LIST"
90 PRINT TAB(14)">>>>>>>>>>>>>"
100 PRINT:PRINT
110 PRINT"This program  stores all the  birthdays"
120 PRINT"you have to remember and will print out"
130 PRINT"all the birthdays  left in  the current"
140 PRINT"year."
150 PRINT:PRINT
160 :
170 REM Read data
180 DIM name$(100),date(100)
190 WHILE name$(index)<>"eof"
200 :   index=index+1
210 :   READ name$(index),date(index)
220 WEND
230 :
240 REM Sort routine
250 index=index-1
260 FOR x=1 TO index-1
270 :   FOR y=x+1 TO index
280 :     IF date(y)<date(x) THEN GOSUB 870:REM Swap
290 :   NEXT
300 NEXT
310 :
320 REM Routine to get date
330 PRINT"Key in today's date in the format MM/DD
340 WHILE LOWER$(RIGHT$(y$,1))<>"y
```

```
350 :    LOCATE 1,18
360 :    PRINT SPACE$(80)
370 :    f=1
380 :    WHILE f=1
390 :       d$=""
400 :       n=0:mm=1:dd=1
410 :       LOCATE 17,15
420 :       PRINT SPACE$(5)
430 :       LOCATE 17,15
440 :       WHILE n<4
450 :          a$=INKEY$:IF a$="" THEN 450
460 :          f=0
470 :          IF ASC(a$)<48 OR ASC(a$)>57 THEN f=1:n=4
480 :          n=n+1
490 :          d$=d$+a$
500 :          IF n=2 AND f=0 THEN mm=VAL(d$)
510 :          IF mm<1 OR mm>12 THEN n=4:f=1
520 :          IF n=4 AND f=0 THEN dd=VAL(RIGHT$(d$,2))
530 :          IF dd=0 OR dd>31 THEN f=1
540 :          IF f=0 THEN PRINT a$;
550 :          IF n=2 AND f=0 THEN PRINT"/";
560 :       WEND
570 :    WEND
580 :    PRINT:PRINT:PRINT
590 :    INPUT "Is this the correct date (y/n)";y$
600 WEND
610 :
620 REM Print out birthdays remaining
630 CLS
640 PRINT"The birthdays remaining this year are:"
650 PRINT:PRINT
660 mnt$="JanFebMarAprMayJunJulAugSepOctNovDec"
670 FOR j=1 TO index
680 :   IF date(j)>=VAL(d$) THEN GOSUB 790:pr=1
690 NEXT
700 IF pr=0 THEN PRINT TAB(8)"No birthdays remaining."
710 PRINT:PRINT
720 PRINT"Press any key to end program."
730 a$=INKEY$:IF a$="" THEN 730
740 CLS
750 END
760 :
770 :
780 REM Print subroutine
790 day=date(j)-100*INT(date(j)/100)
800 mo=INT(date(j)/100)-1
810 mo$=MID$(mnt$,3*mo+1,3)
820 PRINT name$(j);"'s birthday is";day;mo$;"."
830 RETURN
840 :
850 :
860 REM Swap subroutine
870 temp=date(y):temp$=name$(y)
880 date(y)=date(x):name$(y)=name$(x)
890 date(x)=temp:name$(x)=temp$
900 RETURN
910 :
```

```
920 :
930 REM Key in the birthday data in the form name,mmdd
940 REM where mm is the month number and dd the day number.
950 :
960 REM Make the last two elements of data be eof,0
970 :
980 REM Some sample data is given, but to make this a
990 REM useful program you should key in your own list.
1000 :
1010 REM Up to 100 birthdays may be entered in any order.
1020 :
1030 :
1040 DATA Bill Smythe,0812,Jim Smith,1130,Liz Graham,0303
1050 DATA John Gordon,0419,Teresa Gordon,1222
1060 DATA Ian McLean,0421,Anne McLean,0625,Sam Dolan,0517
1070 DATA eof,0
```

P35 Calendar

This program can be used to print out the calendar for any month in the twentieth century.

COMMANDS

Key in the program and RUN.
Enter month and year when requested.

```
10 REM Calendar
20 PAPER 0:INK 0,2
30 PEN 1:INK 1,26
40 BORDER 2
50 MODE 1
60 :
70 PRINT TAB(16)"--------"
80 PRINT TAB(16)"CALENDAR"
90 PRINT TAB(16)"--------"
100 PRINT:PRINT
110 PRINT"This program  can be used to  print the"
120 PRINT"calendar for any month in the twentieth"
130 PRINT"century."
140 PRINT:PRINT
150 INPUT "Name of required month";mth$
160 PRINT
170 INPUT "Year";y%
180 PRINT
190 PRINT"Calculating - please wait"
200 DIM c(6,5)
210 :
220 d$="MonTueWedThuFriSatSun"
230 mth$=LOWER$(mth$)
240 mt=1
250 READ qu$,f,d
260 q$=LOWER$(qu$)
270 :
280 WHILE LEFT$(mth$,3)<>LEFT$(q$,3) AND mt<13
290 :   mt=mt+1
300 :   IF mt<13 THEN READ qu$,f,d
310 :   q$=LOWER$(qu$)
320 WEND
330 :
340 IF mt=13 OR y%>1999 OR y%<1900 THEN RUN
350 REM Invalid entry
360 :
370 y%=y%-1900
380 leap=INT(y%/4)
390 offset=y%+leap
400 IF y%=4*leap AND mt<3 THEN offset=offset-1
410 IF y%=4*leap AND mt=2 THEN d=29
420 offset=offset-INT(offset/7)*7
430 f=f+offset
440 f=f-INT(f/7)*7
```

```
450 IF f=0 THEN f=7
460 :
470 FOR n=0 TO f-2
480 :   c(n,0)=0
490 NEXT
500 :
510 day=1
520 FOR n=f-1 TO 6
530 :   c(n,0)=day
540 :   day=day+1
550 NEXT
560 :
570 FOR j=1 TO 5
580 :   FOR n=0 TO 6
590 :     c(n,j)=day
600 :     day=day+1
610 :     IF day>d THEN j=5:n=6
620 :   NEXT
630 NEXT
640 :
650 CLS
660 LOCATE 9,3
670 PRINT qu$
680 LOCATE 21,3
690 PRINT y%+1900
700 :
710 LOCATE 1,8
720 FOR n=0 TO 6
730 :   PRINT TAB(4);MID$(d$,n*3+1,3)
740 NEXT
750 :
760 FOR j=0 TO 5
770 :   FOR n=0 TO 6
780 :     LOCATE 4*j+11,n+8
790 :     IF c(n,j)<>0 THEN PRINT USING "##";c(n,j)
800 :   NEXT
810 NEXT
820 :
830 a$=INKEY$:IF LEN(a$)=0 THEN 830
840 REM Any key ends program
850 CLS
860 END
870 DATA January,1,31,February,4,28,March,4,31,April,7,30
880 DATA May,2,31,June,5,30,July,7,31,August,3,31
890 DATA September,6,30,October,1,31,November,4,30
900 DATA December,6,31
```

```
                    March 1983

            Mon         7  14 21 28
            Tue     1   8  15 22 29
            Wed     2   9  16 23 30
            Thu     3  10  17 24 31
            Fri     4  11  18 25
            Sat     5  12  19 26
            Sun     6  13  20 27
        >
```

P36   Telephone List

This program allows the user to select a telephone number
from a list held as data statements.

You do not have to enter the full name to select the number.
As long as the string entered is part of one of the names,
then the telephone number is displayed.

COMMANDS

Key in the program and RUN.
Follow instructions.


```
10 REM Telephone list
20 PAPER 0:INK 0,23
30 PEN 1:INK 1,3
40 BORDER 23
50 MODE 1
60 :
70 PRINT TAB(14)"++++++++++++++"
80 PRINT TAB(14)"TELEPHONE LIST"
90 PRINT TAB(14)"++++++++++++++"
100 PRINT:PRINT
110 PRINT"This  program  is  used  as a  personal"
120 PRINT"Telephone directory.  It can hold up to"
130 PRINT"100 names and telephone numbers in data"
140 PRINT"statements.  This information  is keyed"
150 PRINT"in by the user."
160 PRINT
170 PRINT"The program  will  search  through  the"
180 PRINT"database  looking  for a name  input to"
190 PRINT"the computer."
200 PRINT
210 PRINT"A partial match will also give a number."
220 PRINT"For example, if you input  'Bill', then"
230 PRINT"a match  will be  found  for both  Bill"
240 PRINT"Smith and Bill Jones."
250 PRINT:PRINT
260 :
270 REM Read addresses
280 DIM nn$(100,1),nm$(100)
290 WHILE nm$(index)<>"eof"
300 :   index=index+1
310 :   READ nn$(index,0),nn$(index,1)
320 :   nm$(index)=LOWER$(nn$(index,0))
330 WEND
340 index=index-1
350 :
360 PRINT"Press any key to continue."
370 a$=INKEY$:IF a$="" THEN 370
380 :
```

```
390 y$="y"
400 WHILE LOWER$(LEFT$(y$,1))="y"
410 :   CLS
420 :   INPUT "Who's number do you want";name$
430 :   name$=LOWER$(name$)
440 :   la=LEN(name$):found=0
450 :   FOR j=1 TO index
460 :     lb=LEN(nm$(j))
470 :     IF la<=lb THEN GOSUB 590:REM Compare and print
480 :   NEXT
490 :   PRINT:PRINT
500 :   IF found=0 THEN PRINT"We have no number for ";name$;"."
510 :   PRINT:PRINT
520 :   INPUT "Another number (y/n)";y$
530 WEND
540 CLS
550 END
560 :
570 :
580 REM Compare and print subroutine
590 flag=0
600 FOR k=1 TO lb-la
610 :   IF MID$(nm$(j),k,la)=name$ THEN flag=1:found=1
620 NEXT
630 IF flag=1 THEN PRINT nn$(j,0);"'s number is ";nn$(j,1);"."
640 RETURN
650 :
660 :
670 REM Key in data from line 740 onwards.
680 REM Data is in the form 'name,number'
690 REM Ensure the final two data items are eof,0.
700 REM Some sample data is shown.
710 :
720 :
730 DATA Bill Smith,12354,Bill Jones,45678
740 DATA Alice Graham,0101 256 3456
750 DATA John Gordon,East Kilbride 49400
760 DATA Ian McLean,03552 26744,Joe Bloggs,01 222 2225
770 DATA eof,0
```

P37 Investments

This program calculates how much income can be generated from capital if the interest earned by that capital is known.

The user is presented with the choice of increasing his or her income at the expense of reducing capital.

COMMANDS

Key in the program and RUN.


```
10 REM Investments
20 PAPER 0:INK 0,20
30 PEN 1:INK 1,1
40 BORDER 20
50 MODE 1
60 :
70 PRINT TAB(15)"==========="
80 PRINT TAB(15)"INVESTMENTS"
90 PRINT TAB(15)"==========="
100 PRINT:PRINT
110 PRINT"This  program can be used to  plan your"
120 PRINT"future  investments,  provided that you"
130 PRINT"wish  these  investments  to  provide a"
140 PRINT"regular income."
150 :
160 PRINT:PRINT
170 INPUT "Monthly income required";mi
180 PRINT
190 INPUT "Current annual interest rate (%)";rt
200 :
210 ON ERROR GOTO 560
220 CLS
230 rt=rt/100
240 inv=mi*12/rt
250 inv=INT(inv*100+0.5)/100
260 PRINT"An investment of";inv;"will"
270 PRINT"provide a monthly income of";mi
280 PRINT
290 PRINT"Note that no capital has been used."
300 PRINT:PRINT
310 PRINT"If you wish to use up your capital,"
320 PRINT"enter the number of years for which you"
330 PRINT"require an income."
340 PRINT
350 INPUT "How many years";yr%
360 :
370 rt=rt/12
380 t=(1+rt)^(12*yr%)
390 inv=mi*(t-1)/rt/t
```

```
400 inv=INT(inv*100+0.5)/100
410 PRINT
420 PRINT"An investment of";inv;"will"
430 PRINT"provide a monthly income of";mi
440 PRINT"for";yr%;"years."
450 PRINT:PRINT
460 PRINT"Note that no currency units are stated."
470 PRINT"This program works for any currency."
480 PRINT:PRINT
490 PRINT"Press any key to end."
500 a$=INKEY$:IF LEN(a$)=0 THEN 500
510 CLS
520 END
530 :
540 :
550 REM Bad data entered
560 PRINT:PRINT
570 PRINT"Income  calculations  cannot be made on"
580 PRINT"the figures given.  Please  RUN program"
590 PRINT"again."
600 GOTO 480
```

P38 Loan Repayment Schedule

We use this program to try to dissuade ourselves from buying something using a loan from a finance house.

It can be quite illuminating to have a note of the full schedule of repayments for a loan and to see how slowly the amount owed drops.

If the interest rate changes during the period of a loan, then simply RUN the program again as if you had taken out a new loan, with a reduced amount borrowed.

The program allows you to choose either a screen or a printer output.

COMMANDS

Key in the program and RUN.
Follow the instructions.


```
10 REM Loan repayment schedule
20 PAPER 0:INK 0,3
30 PEN 1:INK 1,22
40 BORDER 3
50 MODE 1
60 :
70 PRINT TAB(10)"***********************"
80 PRINT TAB(10)"LOAN REPAYMENT SCHEDULE"
90 PRINT TAB(10)"***********************"
100 PRINT:PRINT
110 PRINT"This  program can  be used to  plan the"
120 PRINT"repayment schedule for a loan. The loan"
130 PRINT"is paid  back at a fixed   monthly rate."
140 PRINT"The interest is also fixed. The program"
150 PRINT"produces a repayment table."
160 PRINT:PRINT
170 PRINT"If you  wish to  use a  printer, ensure"
180 PRINT"that  this is  connected, switched  on,"
190 PRINT"and loaded with paper."
200 PRINT:PRINT
210 PRINT"Press any key when ready."
220 a$=INKEY$:IF LEN(a$)=0 THEN 220
230 :
240 WHILE LOWER$(LEFT$(y$,1))<>"y"
250 :   CLS
260 :   INPUT "What is the amount of the loan";amt
270 :   PRINT
280 :   INPUT "What is the interest/month (%)";it
290 :   PRINT
300 :   INPUT "First repayment month number (1-12)";mth%
```

```
310 :   PRINT
320 :   INPUT "What is the monthly repayment";rep
330 :   PRINT
340 :   INPUT "What year is it";yr%
350 :   PRINT:PRINT
360 :   PRINT"Please check your entries careflly.  In"
370 :   PRINT"this  program  silly  entries will give"
380 :   PRINT"silly results."
390 :   PRINT
400 :   INPUT "Are the above entries correct (y/n)";y$
410 WEND
420 :
430 WHILE a<>3
440 :   CLS
450 :   PRINT"Select output device by pressing:"
460 :   PRINT:PRINT
470 :   PRINT TAB(8)"Key 1 - Screen"
480 :   PRINT
490 :   PRINT TAB(8)"Key 2 - Printer"
500 :   PRINT
510 :   PRINT TAB(8)"Key 3 - Ends program
520 :   a$=INKEY$:IF a$<>"1" AND a$<>"2" AND a$<>"3" THEN 520
530 :   a=VAL(a$)
540 :   ON a GOSUB 620,680
550 WEND
560 CLS
570 ZONE 13
580 END
590 :
600 :
610 REM Screen
620 cha=0
630 GOSUB 740
640 RETURN
650 :
660 :
670 REM Printer
680 cha=8
690 GOSUB 740
700 RETURN
710 :
720 :
730 REM Print results
740 CLS
750 ZONE 10
760 PRINT #cha,"Year","Month","Amount","Amount"
770 PRINT #cha,TAB(21)"paid","owed"
780 PRINT #cha,"----","-----","------","------"
790 IF mth%>12 THEN mth%=12
800 IF mth%<1 THEN mth%=1
810 y%=yr%:m%=mth%:am=amt:pd=0
820 WHILE am>0
830 :   m%=m%+1
840 :   IF m%=13 THEN m%=1:y%=y%+1
850 :   am=am*(1+it/100)
860 :   am=am-rep
870 :   pd=pd+rep
```

```
880 :   IF am<0 THEN pd=pd+am:am=0
890 :   p$="#### ######### ########.## ######.##"
900 :   PRINT #cha, USING p$;y%;m%;pd;am
910 WEND
920 PRINT:PRINT
930 PRINT"Press any key for menu."
940 a$=INKEY$:IF LEN(a$)=0 THEN 940
950 RETURN
```

Year	Month	Amount paid	Amount owed
1986	5	200.00	2860.00
1986	6	400.00	2717.20
1986	7	600.00	2571.54
1986	8	800.00	2422.97
1986	9	1000.00	2271.43
1986	10	1200.00	2116.86
1986	11	1400.00	1959.20
1986	12	1600.00	1798.38
1987	1	1800.00	1634.35
1987	2	2000.00	1467.04
1987	3	2200.00	1296.38
1987	4	2400.00	1122.31
1987	5	2600.00	944.75
1987	6	2800.00	763.65
1987	7	3000.00	578.92
1987	8	3200.00	390.50
1987	9	3400.00	198.31
1987	10	3600.00	2.28
1987	11	3602.32	0.00

P39 Interference

This program generates an interference type pattern. This is repeated for a variety of foreground and background colours.

COMMANDS

Key in the program and RUN.

```
10 REM Interference
20 MODE 2
30 PAPER 0
40 PEN 1
50 FOR col=0 TO 25
60 :    INK 0,col
70 :    CLS
80 :    BORDER col
90 :    INK 1,25-col
100 :   stp%=3+6*RND(1)
110 :
120 :   FOR X=0 TO 639 STEP stp%
130 :     PLOT X,0
140 :     DRAW 639-X,399
150 :   NEXT
160 :
170 :   FOR Y=0 TO 399 STEP stp%
180 :     PLOT 0,Y
190 :     DRAW 639,399-Y
200 :   NEXT
210 :
220 FOR del=0 TO 200:NEXT
230 NEXT
240 RUN
```

P40 Drawing Circles

This program shows the user three different methods of drawing circles on the Amstrad screen.

COMMANDS

Key in the program and RUN.
Follow instructions.


```
100 REM Program - Drawing Circles
110 MODE 1
120 t$="y"
130 DIM sinp(63),cosp(63)
140 FOR i=1 TO 63
150    sinp(i)=SIN(i*0.1)
160    cosp(i)=COS(i*0.1)
170 NEXT i
180 WHILE t$="y" OR t$="Y"
190    MODE 1
200    PRINT : PRINT : PRINT
210    PRINT "            CIRCLES"
220    PRINT : PRINT
230    PRINT "This program can be used to show the"
240    PRINT "various ways of drawing circles with"
250    PRINT "the AMSTRAD.  The methods available"
260    PRINT "are:" : PRINT : PRINT
270    PRINT "1. Short line segments round the edge"
280    PRINT "2. Dots distributed round the edge"
290    PRINT "3. Shaded circle using dots"
300    PRINT:PRINT:PRINT
310    PRINT "Make a selection to see effect"
320    s=0
330    WHILE s<1 OR s>3
340       s$=INKEY$:IF s$="" THEN 340
350       s=VAL(s$)
360    WEND
370    MODE 2
380    ORIGIN 320,200
390    r=150
400    ON s GOSUB 470,530,590
410    LOCATE 1,24:PRINT "Another go (Y/N)
420    t$=INKEY$:IF t$="" THEN 420
430 WEND
440 MODE 1
450 END
460 REM Short Lines
470 MOVE r,0
480 FOR i=1 TO 63
490    DRAW r*cosp(i),r*sinp(i)
500 NEXT i
```

```
510 RETURN
520 REM Dots
530 PLOT r,0
540 FOR i=1 TO 63
550    PLOT r*cosp(i),r*sinp(i)
560 NEXT i
570 RETURN
580 REM Shaded
590 ill=0.7:REM change this line to change shading
600 length=2*r
610 lines=length*ill
620 dx=2*r/lines
630 x=r+dx
640 WHILE x>-(r+dx)
650    x=x-dx
660    t=r*r-x*x
670    IF t>0 THEN y=SQR(t) ELSE y=0
680    GOSUB 710
690 WEND
700 REM Line shading
710 dist=2*y
720 dots=dist*ill
730 IF dots=0 THEN dots=1
740 dy=2*y/dots
750 FOR k=1 TO dots
760    j=-y+k*dy
770    PLOT x,j
780 NEXT k
790 RETURN
```

P41 Interfering Circles

It takes a little time for this program to finish, but we think that the effect is quite pretty.

COMMANDS

Key in the program and RUN.


```
10   REM INTERFERING CIRCLES
20   REM A DEMONSTRATION PROGRAM
30   MODE 0
40   PRINT CHR$(22)+CHR$(1)
50   LOCATE 10,10
60   PRINT "SETTING UP .";
70   DIM sinp(63),cosp(63)
80   FOR I%=1 TO 63
90     sinp(I%)=SIN(I%*0.1)
100    cosp(I%)=COS(I%*0.1)
110      PRINT ".";
120  NEXT I%
130  :
140  MODE 0
150  ST=4
160  FOR Y=10 TO 200 STEP ST
170    C=0:GOSUB 300
180    C=1:GOSUB 300
190  NEXT Y
200  :
210  K=1
220  WHILE 1=1
230    FOR I=1 TO 8
240      INK I,I+K MOD 8
250    NEXT I
260    K=K+1 MOD 8
270  WEND
280  END
290  :
300  REM CIRCLE DRAWING SUBROUTINE
310  ORIGIN 200+C*200,200
320  P=0:MOVE 0,Y
330  FOR I%=1 TO 63
340    DRAW Y*sinp(I%),Y*cosp(I%), (Y/ST) MOD 8
350  NEXT I%
360  RETURN
```

P42 Shading

This program uses the PLOT command to draw a line by placing a series of dots along it. The density of the dots gives a measure of the illumination of the line.

The points on the line are calculated by using the formula:

$$Y=M*X+C.$$

This formula leads to the following rules for calculating M and C.

$$M=(Y2-Y1)/(X2-X1)$$
$$C=Y2-M*X2$$

where X1,Y1 and X2,Y2 are two points on the line. These rules fall down when the line is vertical and the program has a small adjustment when this situation arises.

COMMANDS

Key in the program and RUN.
Follow instructions.


```
10 REM Program - Line Shading
20 MODE 1
30 PRINT "          LINE SHADING"
40 PRINT:PRINT
50 PRINT "This program uses the PLOT command"
60 PRINT "to show the effect of 'shading' a line."
70 PRINT "The effect of shading is achieved by"
80 PRINT "placing a series of dots along the line."
90 PRINT "The number of dots corresponds to the "
100 PRINT "illumination of the line."
110 PRINT:PRINT
120 PRINT "The line is drawn in MODE 2, thus with"
130 PRINT "only two colours.":PRINT
140 PRINT "The line is drawn between the points"
150 PRINT "X1,Y1 and X2,Y2 with an illumination "
160 PRINT "constant between .05 and .9."
170 PRINT
180 INPUT "Enter first point ",X1,Y1
190 INPUT "Enter second point ",X2,Y2
200 INPUT "Enter illumination constant ",I
210 MODE 2:BORDER 9
220 GOSUB 1000
230 END
1000 REM SUBROUTINE TO DRAW LINE
1010 REM INPUTS X1,X2,Y1,Y2,I
1020 REM DATA NAMES USED:
```

```
1030 REM        M-GRADIENT
1040 REM        C-INTERCEPT
1050 REM        dist-length of line
1060 REM        dots-number of dots
1070 REM        dx-distance between dots
1080 REM        k- counter
1090 :
1100 REM validate data
1110 IF X1<0 OR X1>640 THEN PRINT "Error in X1":RETURN
1120 IF X2<0 OR X2>640 THEN PRINT "Error in X2":RETURN
1130 IF Y1<0 OR Y1>400 THEN PRINT "Error in Y1":RETURN
1140 IF Y2<0 OR Y2>400 THEN PRINT "Error in Y2":RETURN
1150 IF X1=X2 THEN GOTO 1500
1160 M=(Y2-Y1)/(X2-X1)
1170 C=Y1-M*X1
1180 dist=SQR((X1-X2)^2+(Y2-Y1)^2)
1190 dots=dist*I
1200 dx=(X2-X1)/dots
1210 FOR k=1 TO dots
1220    j=X1+k*dx
1230    PLOT j,M*j+C
1240 NEXT k
1250 RETURN
1500 REM vertical line
1510 d=ABS(Y2-Y1)
1520 N=d*I
1530 IF Y2<Y1 THEN T=Y2:Y2=Y1:Y1=T
1540 DY=(Y2-Y1)/N
1550 FOR k=1 TO N
1560    j=Y1+k*DY
1570    PLOT X1,j
1580 NEXT k
1590 RETURN
```

P43 Translation

To translate, or to move a line, we must compute the new end points of the line and then draw it.

If we can move a single line, then we have the capability of moving line drawings about the screen.

To move a line we must know the end points of the original line and the distance to be moved in both the X and Y directions.

The program uses the shading routine developed earlier to redraw the line.

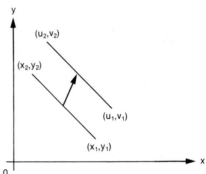

COMMANDS

Key in the program and RUN.
Follow instructions.

```
100 REM Program - Translation
110 MODE 1
120 PRINT "          TRANSLATION"
130 PRINT:PRINT:PRINT
140 PRINT "This program introduces a simple"
150 PRINT "mechanism for changeing the position"
160 PRINT "of a line.  If you have a routine for"
170 PRINT "moveing single lines then you can move"
180 PRINT "complete line drawings about the screen"
190 PRINT "at your own convenience."
200 PRINT
210 PRINT "To move a line we must know its original"
220 PRINT "position and the distance to be"
230 PRINT "traversed in both the X and Y directions"
240 :
250 INPUT "Enter the first end point of the line ",X1,Y1
260 INPUT "Enter the second end point of the line ",X2,Y2
270 INPUT "Enter the illumination constant ",I
280 INPUT "Enter the X-direction movement ",K1
290 INPUT "Enter the Y-direction movement ",K2
300 MODE 2:BORDER 9
```

```
310 GOSUB 1000
320 GOSUB 2000
330 END
1000 REM SUBROUTINE TO DRAW LINE
1010 REM INPUTS X1,X2,Y1,Y2,I
1020 REM DATA NAMES USED:
1030 REM      M-GRADIENT
1040 REM      C-INTERCEPT
1050 REM      dist,d-length of line
1060 REM      dots,N-number of dots
1070 REM      dx,DY-distance between dots
1080 REM      k- counter
1090 REM      T,j - temporary variables
1100 REM validate data
1110 IF X1<0 OR X1>640 THEN PRINT "Error in X1":RETURN
1120 IF X2<0 OR X2>640 THEN PRINT "Error in X2":RETURN
1130 IF Y1<0 OR Y1>400 THEN PRINT "Error in Y1":RETURN
1140 IF Y2<0 OR Y2>400 THEN PRINT "Error in Y2":RETURN
1150 IF X1=X2 THEN GOTO 1500
1160 M=(Y2-Y1)/(X2-X1)
1170 C=Y1-M*X1
1180 dist=SQR((X1-X2)^2+(Y2-Y1)^2)
1190 dots=dist*I
1200 dx=(X2-X1)/dots
1210 FOR k=1 TO dots
1220    j=X1+k*dx
1230    PLOT j,M*j+C
1240 NEXT k
1250 RETURN
1500 REM vertical line
1510 d=ABS(Y2-Y1)
1520 N=d*I
1530 IF Y2<Y1 THEN T=Y2:Y2=Y1:Y1=T
1540 DY=(Y2-Y1)/N
1550 FOR k=1 TO N
1560    j=Y1+k*DY
1570    PLOT X1,j
1580 NEXT k
1590 RETURN
2000 REM Routine to translate line
2010 REM Variables used:
2020 REM      X1,Y1,X2,Y2 end points
2030 REM      K1,K2 movements
2040 :
2050 X1=X1+K1:Y1=Y1+K2
2060 X2=X2+K1:Y2=Y2+K2
2070 GOSUB 1000
2080 RETURN
```

P44 Parallelogram

Using the routines developed in the previous programs we can shade a parallelogram.

The parallelogram is drawn by taking a vector (a straight line) and moving it to a new position, drawing many intermediate lines between the starting and finishing vectors. As before we use the shading routine to mimic illumination.

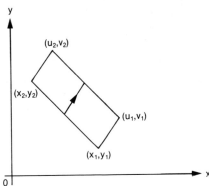

COMMANDS

Key in the program and RUN.
Follow instructions.

```
100 REM Program - Parallelogram
110 MODE 1
120 PRINT "              PARALLELOGRAM"
130 PRINT
140 PRINT "This program uses the routines developed";
150 PRINT "in the previous programs to shade a "
160 PRINT "parallelogram. As pointed in the"
170 PRINT "description, we can now specify "
180 PRINT "illumination in two directions to "
190 PRINT "produce variable shading.":PRINT
200 PRINT "To draw the parallelogram we need to"
210 PRINT "know the generating vector position and"
220 PRINT "the distance to be traversed in both "
230 PRINT "the X and Y directions."
240 PRINT
250 INPUT "Enter the first end point of the line ",P1,Q1
260 INPUT "Enter the second end point of the line ",P2,Q2
270 INPUT "Enter the X-illumination constant ",I1
275 INPUT "Enter the Y-illumination constant ",I2
280 INPUT "Enter the X-direction movement ",C1
290 INPUT "Enter the Y-direction movement ",C2
300 MODE 2:BORDER 9
310 GOSUB 3000
```

```
 320 END
1000 REM SUBROUTINE TO DRAW LINE
1010 REM INPUTS X1,X2,Y1,Y2,I
1020 REM DATA NAMES USED:
1030 REM      M-GRADIENT
1040 REM      C-INTERCEPT
1050 REM      dist,d-length of line
1060 REM      dots,N-number of dots
1070 REM      dx,DY-distance between dots
1080 REM      k- counter
1090 REM      T,j - temporary variables
1100 REM validate data
1110 IF X1<0 OR X1>640 THEN PRINT "Error in X1":RETURN
1120 IF X2<0 OR X2>640 THEN PRINT "Error in X2":RETURN
1130 IF Y1<0 OR Y1>400 THEN PRINT "Error in Y1":RETURN
1140 IF Y2<0 OR Y2>400 THEN PRINT "Error in Y2":RETURN
1150 IF X1=X2 THEN GOTO 1500
1160 M=(Y2-Y1)/(X2-X1)
1170 C=Y1-M*X1
1180 dist=SQR((X1-X2)^2+(Y2-Y1)^2)
1190 dots=dist*I:IF dots=0 THEN dots=1
1200 dx=(X2-X1)/dots
1210 FOR k=1 TO dots
1220    j=X1+k*dx
1230    PLOT j,M*j+C
1240 NEXT k
1250 RETURN
1500 REM vertical line
1510 d=ABS(Y2-Y1)
1520 N=d*I
1530 IF Y2<Y1 THEN T=Y2:Y2=Y1:Y1=T
1540 DY=(Y2-Y1)/N
1550 FOR k=1 TO N
1560    j=Y1+k*DY
1570    PLOT X1,j
1580 NEXT k
1590 RETURN
2000 REM Routine to translate line
2010 REM Variables used:
2020 REM      X1,Y1,X2,Y2 end points
2030 REM      K1,K2 movements
2040 :
2050 X1=X1+K1:Y1=Y1+K2
2060 X2=X2+K1:Y2=Y2+K2
2070 GOSUB 1000
2080 RETURN
3000 REM Parallelogram routine
3010 REM Routine to sketch parallelogram
3020 REM Variables used:
3030 REM
3100 X1=P1:X2=P2:Y1=Q1:Y2=Q2
3110 GOSUB 1000
3120 length=SQR(C1*C1+C2*C2)
3130 lines=length*I2
3140 dC1=C1/lines
3150 dC2=C2/lines
3160 FOR L=1 TO lines
```

```
3170    X1=P1:X2=P2:Y1=Q1:Y2=Q2:I=I1
3180    K1=L*dC1:K2=L*dC2
3190    GOSUB 2000
3200 NEXT L
3210 RETURN
```

P45   Shape Grabber

When dealing with line drawings one needs to know only the end points of each line and the method of drawing the lines. The end points of the lines can be held in a two dimensional array, and there are various methods of drawing the lines.

It can help to have a rough drawing of your object before running the program.

COMMANDS

Key in the program and RUN.
Follow instructions, and enter your line drawing one line at a time.


```
100 REM Program - Shape Grabber
110 DEF FNcheckx(X)=(X>0) AND (X<640)
120 DEF FNchecky(Y)=(Y>0) AND (Y<400)
130 MODE 1
140 PRINT:PRINT:PRINT
150 PRINT "This program is used to draw shapes"
160 PRINT "in MODE 0.  The shape is recorded as an"
170 PRINT "array of points, which when joined"
180 PRINT "together form a line drawing.  The "
190 PRINT "picture is stored as a series of end"
200 PRINT "points of the lines.  The number of"
210 PRINT "lines in the drawing are stored as the"
220 PRINT "first element of the array."
230 PRINT:PRINT:PRINT:
240 PRINT "Press any key to enter figure"
250 z$=INKEY$:IF z$="" THEN 250
260 :
270 CLS
280 PRINT:PRINT
290 INPUT "Number of lines in shape=",n
300 DIM shape(2,2*n)
310 REM enter shape
320 FOR i=1 TO 2*n STEP 2
330    flag=0
340    WHILE flag=0
350       CLS
360       PRINT "Now enter the endpoints of line number":
          PRINT (i+1)/2
370       LOCATE 1,6
380       INPUT "Enter end point (X,Y) ",
              shape(1,i),shape(2,i)
390       INPUT "Enter other end point ",
              shape(1,i+1),shape(2,i+1)
400       flag=FNcheckx(shape(1,i))
              AND FNcheckx(shape(1,i+1))
```

```
410      flag=flag*(FNchecky(shape(2,i))
            AND FNchecky(shape(2,i+1)))
420      IF flag=0 THEN LOCATE 1,20:PRINT "Error"+CHR$(7)
            ELSE 450
430      PRINT "Press key to reenter"
440      z$=INKEY$:IF z$="" THEN 440
450    WEND
460 NEXT i
470 REM draw shape
480 LOCATE 1,20: PRINT "Press any key to see shape"
490 z$=INKEY$:IF z$="" THEN 490
500 MODE 0
510 FOR i=1 TO 2*n STEP 2
520    MOVE shape(1,i),shape(2,i)
530    DRAW shape(1,i+1),shape(2,i+1)
540 NEXT i
550 z$=INKEY$:IF z$="" THEN 550
560 MODE 1
```

P46 Rotation

This program uses the shape grabbing routine to get a user defined shape. The shape is then rotated through an angle of PI/2 radians, the screen is cleared and the new view is shown.

The program shows the advantage of using arrays to process shapes. The rotation problem is reduced to that of matrix (array) multiplication.

COMMANDS

Key in the program and RUN.
Enter coordinates when prompted.
Press any key to rotate figure.


```
100 REM Program - Rotation
110 DEF FNcheckx(X)=(X>-320) AND (X<320)
120 DEF FNchecky(Y)=(Y>-200) AND (Y<200)
130 MODE 1
140 GOSUB 1000:REM get shape
145 MODE 0:ORIGIN 320,200
150 GOSUB 2000:REM draw shape
160 LOCATE 1,20:PRINT "press key to rotate"
170 z$=INKEY$:IF z$="" THEN 170
180 GOSUB 3000:REM rotate shape
190 GOSUB 2000:REM draw shape
200 z$=INKEY$:IF z$="" THEN 200
210 END
980 :
990 REM shape grabbing subroutine
1000 CLS
1010 PRINT:PRINT
1020 INPUT "Number of lines in shape=",n
1030 DIM shape(2,2*n)
1040 REM enter shape
1050 FOR i=1 TO 2*n STEP 2
1060    flag=0
1070    WHILE flag=0
1080       CLS
1090       PRINT "Now enter the endpoints of line number":
             PRINT (i+1)/2
1100       LOCATE 1,6
1110       INPUT "Enter end point (X,Y) ",
             shape(1,i),shape(2,i)
1120       INPUT "Enter other end point ",
             shape(1,i+1),shape(2,i+1)
1130       flag=FNcheckx(shape(1,i))
             AND FNcheckx(shape(1,i+1))
```

```
1140       flag=flag*(FNchecky(shape(2,i))
               AND FNchecky(shape(2,i+1)))
1150       IF flag=0 THEN LOCATE 1,20:PRINT "Error"+CHR$(7)
               ELSE 1180
1160       PRINT "Press key to reenter"
1170       z$=INKEY$:IF z$="" THEN 1170
1180    WEND
1190 NEXT i
1200 RETURN
1970 :
1980 :
1990 REM shape drawing routine
2000 MOVE 0,0
2010 FOR i=1 TO 2*n STEP 2
2020   MOVE shape(1,i),shape(2,i)
2030   DRAW shape(1,i+1),shape(2,i+1)
2040 NEXT i
2050 RETURN
2970 REM Rotation subroutine
2980 REM Old shape in shape(x,y)
2990 REM new shape in nshape(x,y)
3000 FOR i=1 TO 2*n
3010   t=shape(1,i)
3015   shape(1,i)=-shape(2,i)
3020   shape(2,i)=t
3030 NEXT i
3040 RETURN
```

P47 Transformations

This program uses the shape grabbing routine to allow the user to enter a line drawing, and this is then displayed on the screen.

The user can then use the program to perform various transformations on the line drawing.

The program informs the user of the options available.

COMMANDS

Key in the program and RUN.
Follow instructions.

This program first of all allows the user to enter a shape. The user then chooses which transformation to put the shape through. The choices are :

I-Identity	R-Reflection in y=x
H-Half turn	X-Reflection in x-axis
Q-Quarter	Y-Reflection in y-axis
turn	B-Back quarter turn

Note that a single letter suffices.

```
100 REM Program - Tranformations
110 DEF FNcheckx(X)=(X>-320) AND (X<320)
120 DEF FNchecky(Y)=(Y>-200) AND (Y<200)
130 MODE 1
140 GOSUB 1000:REM get shape
145 MODE 2:ORIGIN 320,200
150 GOSUB 2000:REM draw shape
160 r$=""
170 WHILE r$<>"z"
180    LOCATE 1,25:
       PRINT "Press from 'IRHXQYB' to continue"
190    r$=INKEY$:IF r$="" THEN 190
200    IF ASC(r$)>96 AND ASC(r$)<123
          THEN r$=CHR$(ASC(r$)-32)
210    r=INSTR("IRHXQYB",r$)
220    IF r=0 THEN r$="z":GOTO 270
230    ON r GOSUB
          5100,5200,5300,5400,5500,5600,5700
240    GOSUB 4000:REM undraw shape
250    GOSUB 3000:REM compute new shape
260    GOSUB 2000:REM draw shape
270 WEND
280 END
980 :
990 REM shape grabbing subroutine
1000 CLS
```

```
1010 PRINT:PRINT
1020 INPUT "Number of lines in shape=",n
1030 DIM shape(2,2*n)
1040 REM enter shape
1050 FOR i=1 TO 2*n STEP 2
1060    flag=0
1070    WHILE flag=0
1080       CLS
1090       PRINT "Now enter the endpoints of line number":
             PRINT (i+1)/2
1100       LOCATE 1,6
1110       INPUT "Enter end point (X,Y) ",
                  shape(1,i),shape(2,i)
1120       INPUT "Enter other end point ",
                  shape(1,i+1),shape(2,i+1)
1130       flag=FNcheckx(shape(1,i))
                  AND FNcheckx(shape(1,i+1))
1140       flag=flag*(FNchecky(shape(2,i))
                  AND FNchecky(shape(2,i+1)))
1150       IF flag=0 THEN LOCATE 1,20:PRINT "Error"+CHR$(7)
                  ELSE 1180
1160       PRINT "Press key to reenter"
1170       z$=INKEY$:IF z$="" THEN 1170
1180    WEND
1190 NEXT i
1200 RETURN
1970 :
1980 :
1990 REM shape drawing routine
2000 MOVE 0,0
2010 FOR i=1 TO 2*n STEP 2
2020    MOVE shape(1,i),shape(2,i)
2030    DRAW shape(1,i+1),shape(2,i+1),1
2040 NEXT i
2050 RETURN
2970 REM Rotation subroutine
2980 REM Old shape in shape(x,y)
2990 REM new shape in nshape(x,y)
3000 FOR i=1 TO 2*n
3010    t1=shape(1,i):t2=shape(2,i)
3015    shape(1,i)=r(1,1)*t1+r(1,2)*t2
3020    shape(2,i)=r(2,1)*t1+r(2,2)*t2
3030 NEXT i
3040 RETURN
3970 :
3980 :
3990 REM shape un-drawing routine
4000 FOR i=1 TO 2*n STEP 2
4020    MOVE shape(1,i),shape(2,i)
4030    DRAW shape(1,i+1),shape(2,i+1),0
4040 NEXT i
4050 RETURN
4970 :
4980 :
4990 REM Compute transform array
5100 r(1,1)=1:r(1,2)=0:r(2,1)=0:r(2,2)=1:RETURN
5200 r(1,1)=0:r(1,2)=1:r(2,1)=1:r(2,2)=0:RETURN
```

```
5300  r(1,1)=-1:r(1,2)=0:r(2,1)=0:r(2,2)=-1:RETURN
5400  r(1,1)=1:r(1,2)=0:r(2,1)=0:r(2,2)=-1:RETURN
5500  r(1,1)=0:r(1,2)=-1:r(2,1)=1:r(2,2)=0:RETURN
5600  r(1,1)=-1:r(1,2)=0:r(2,1)=0:r(2,2)=1:RETURN
5700  r(1,1)=0:r(1,2)=1:r(2,1)=-1:r(2,2)=0:RETURN
```

P48 General Transformation

This program allows the user to enter a shape and then to rotate it round the origin.

COMMANDS

Key in the program and RUN.

This program first of all allows the user to enter a shape, then to enter the angle of rotation of the transformation to be executed.

```
100 REM Program - General Transformation
110 DEF FNcheckx(X)=(X>-320) AND (X<320)
120 DEF FNchecky(Y)=(Y>-200) AND (Y<200)
130 MODE 1
140 GOSUB 1000:REM get shape
145 MODE 2:ORIGIN 320,200
150 GOSUB 2000:REM draw shape
160 r$="":DEG
170 WHILE r$<>"z"
180    LOCATE 1,25
190    INPUT "Enter rotation angle (degrees) ",theta
200    LOCATE 1,25:PRINT SPACE$(80);
210    GOSUB 5000:REM compute rotation matrix
220    GOSUB 4000:REM undraw shape
230    GOSUB 3000:REM compute new shape
240    GOSUB 2000:REM draw shape
250    LOCATE 1,25:
       PRINT "Press z to stop, any other to repeat"
260    r$=INKEY$:IF r$="" THEN 260
270    IF r$="Z" THEN r$="z"
280    LOCATE 1,25:PRINT SPACE$(80);
290 WEND
300 END
980 :
990 REM shape grabbing subroutine
1000 CLS
1010 PRINT:PRINT
1020 INPUT "Number of lines in shape=",n
1030 DIM shape(2,2*n)
1040 REM enter shape
1050 FOR i=1 TO 2*n STEP 2
1060    flag=0
1070    WHILE flag=0
1080       CLS
1090       PRINT "Now enter the endpoints of line number":
          PRINT (i+1)/2
1100       LOCATE 1,6
1110       INPUT "Enter end point (X,Y) ",
             shape(1,i),shape(2,i)
```

```
1120      INPUT "Enter other end point ",
              shape(1,i+1),shape(2,i+1)
1130      flag=FNcheckx(shape(1,i))
              AND FNcheckx(shape(1,i+1))
1140      flag=flag*(FNchecky(shape(2,i))
              AND FNchecky(shape(2,i+1)))
1150      IF flag=0 THEN LOCATE 1,20:PRINT "Error"+CHR$(7)
              ELSE 1180
1160      PRINT "Press key to reenter"
1170      z$=INKEY$:IF z$="" THEN 1170
1180    WEND
1190 NEXT i
1200 RETURN
1970 :
1980 :
1990 REM shape drawing routine
2000 MOVE 0,0
2010 FOR i=1 TO 2*n STEP 2
2020    MOVE shape(1,i),shape(2,i)
2030    DRAW shape(1,i+1),shape(2,i+1),1
2040 NEXT i
2050 RETURN
2970 REM Rotation subroutine
2980 REM Old shape in shape(x,y)
2990 REM new shape in nshape(x,y)
3000 FOR i=1 TO 2*n
3010    t1=shape(1,i):t2=shape(2,i)
3015    shape(1,i)=r(1,1)*t1+r(1,2)*t2
3020    shape(2,i)=r(2,1)*t1+r(2,2)*t2
3030 NEXT i
3040 RETURN
3970 :
3980 :
3990 REM shape un-drawing routine
4000 FOR i=1 TO 2*n STEP 2
4020    MOVE shape(1,i),shape(2,i)
4030    DRAW shape(1,i+1),shape(2,i+1),0
4040 NEXT i
4050 RETURN
4970 :
4980 :
4990 REM Compute transform array
5000 r(1,1)=COS(theta):r(1,2)=-SIN(theta)
5010 r(2,1)=SIN(theta):r(2,2)=COS(theta)
5020 RETURN
```

P49   3D Rotation – 1

The object of this program is to rotate a two dimensional shape in the plane of the screen.

The shape chosen is a regular polygon. (Note that in the limit the polygon becomes a circle.)

The polygon is centred at the point X0,Y0,Z0 and has NS sides.

The program uses the ideas of the rotation program presented earlier.

The polygon has a maximum of 10 sides. When this number of sides is chosen, we almost have a circle; so in the limit the routine will form a view of a sphere.

COMMANDS

Key in the program and RUN.
Follow instructions.

```
100 REM Program - 3D Rotation 1
110 MODE 1
120 PRINT:PRINT:PRINT
130 PRINT "The object of this program is to form"
140 PRINT "a three dimensional object in the plane"
150 PRINT "of the screen.  The coordinates of the"
160 PRINT "shape are held in the array s(3,50)."
170 PRINT "Note that the two dimensional shape"
180 PRINT "has a maximum of 50 sides.  The shape"
190 PRINT "is a polygon, and a polygon with 50 "
200 PRINT "sides is almost a circle, so in the"
210 PRINT "limit we will form a sphere."
220 PRINT:PRINT:PRINT
230 PRINT "The polygon is centred at the origin"
240 PRINT "and has N sides."
250 PRINT:PRINT
260 PRINT "Press any key to continue"
270 z$=INKEY$:IF z$="" THEN 270
280 CLS
290 DIM s(3,50),ns(3,50),c(3,3)
300 INPUT "Enter polygon radius ",r
310 INPUT "Enter number of sides ",n
320 INPUT "Enter y-axis rotation (degs) ",beta
330 beta=beta*PI/180
340 MODE 2
350 ORIGIN 320,200
360 theta=beta
370 GOSUB 4000
380 GOSUB 1000:REM get shape
390 GOSUB 3000:REM draw shape
```

```
400 WHILE theta<2*PI+beta
410   GOSUB 2000:REM new view
420   GOSUB 3000:REM draw it
430   theta=theta+beta
440 WEND
450 END
460 :
470 :
990 REM Shape procedure
1000 dalpha=2*PI/n
1010 alpha=-dalpha
1020 FOR i=1 TO n
1030   alpha=alpha+dalpha
1040   s(1,i)=r*COS(alpha)
1050   s(2,i)=r*SIN(alpha)
1060   s(3,i)=0
1070 NEXT i
1080 RETURN
1090 :
1100 :
1990 REM New view procedure
2000 FOR i=1 TO n
2010   ns(1,i)=s(1,i)*c(1,1)+s(2,i)*c(2,1)+s(3,i)*c(3,1)
2020   ns(2,i)=s(1,i)*c(1,2)+s(2,i)*c(2,2)+s(3,i)*c(3,2)
2030   ns(3,i)=s(1,i)*c(1,3)+s(2,i)*c(2,3)+s(3,i)*c(3,3)
2040 NEXT i
2050 FOR j=1 TO n
2060   FOR k=1 TO 3
2070     s(k,j)=ns(k,j)
2080   NEXT k
2090 NEXT j
2100 RETURN
2110 :
2120 :
2990 REM drawing procedure
3000 MOVE s(1,1),s(2,1)
3010 FOR i=2 TO n
3020   DRAW s(1,i),s(2,i)
3030 NEXT i
3040 DRAW s(1,1),s(2,1)
3050 RETURN
3060 :
3070 :
3990 REM y-rotation matrix procedure
4000 c(1,1)=COS(theta)
4010 c(1,2)=0
4020 c(1,3)=-SIN(theta)
4030 c(2,1)=0
4040 c(2,2)=1
4050 c(2,3)=0
4060 c(3,1)=SIN(theta)
4070 c(3,2)=0
4080 c(3,3)=COS(theta)
4090 RETURN
4100 :
4110 :
```

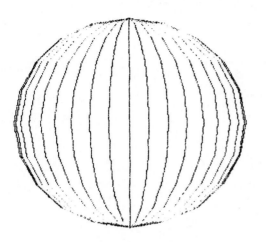

P50　3D Rotation – 2

This program allows the user to enter a polygon and rotate it about the x-axis.

COMMANDS

Key in program and RUN.
Follow instructions.

```
100 REM Program - 3D Rotation 2
110 MODE 1
120 PRINT:PRINT:PRINT
130 PRINT "The object of this program is to form"
140 PRINT "a three dimensional object in the plane"
150 PRINT "of the screen.  The coordinates of the"
160 PRINT "shape are held in the array s(3,50)."
170 PRINT "Note that the two dimensional shape"
180 PRINT "has a maximum of 50 sides.  The shape"
190 PRINT "is a polygon, and a polygon with 50 "
200 PRINT "sides is almost a circle, so in the"
210 PRINT "limit we will form a sphere."
220 PRINT:PRINT:PRINT
230 PRINT "The polygon is centred at the origin"
240 PRINT "and has N sides."
250 PRINT:PRINT
260 PRINT "Press any key to continue"
270 z$=INKEY$:IF z$="" THEN 270
280 CLS
290 DIM s(3,50),ns(3,50),c(3,3)
300 INPUT "Enter polygon radius ",r
310 INPUT "Enter number of sides ",n
320 INPUT "Enter y-axis rotation (degs) ",beta
330 beta=beta*PI/180
340 MODE 2
350 ORIGIN 320,200
360 theta=beta
370 GOSUB 4000
380 GOSUB 1000:REM get shape
390 GOSUB 3000:REM draw shape
400 WHILE theta<2*PI+beta
410    GOSUB 2000:REM new view
420    GOSUB 3000:REM draw it
430    theta=theta+beta
440 WEND
450 END
460 :
470 :
990 REM Shape procedure
1000 dalpha=2*PI/n
1010 alpha=-dalpha
1020 FOR i=1 TO n
```

```
1030    alpha=alpha+dalpha
1040    s(1,i)=r*COS(alpha)
1050    s(2,i)=r*SIN(alpha)
1060    s(3,i)=0
1070 NEXT i
1080 RETURN
1090 :
1100 :
1990 REM New view procedure
2000 FOR i=1 TO n
2010    ns(1,i)=s(1,i)*c(1,1)+s(2,i)*c(2,1)+s(3,i)*c(3,1)
2020    ns(2,i)=s(1,i)*c(1,2)+s(2,i)*c(2,2)+s(3,i)*c(3,2)
2030    ns(3,i)=s(1,i)*c(1,3)+s(2,i)*c(2,3)+s(3,i)*c(3,3)
2040 NEXT i
2050 FOR j=1 TO n
2060    FOR k=1 TO 3
2070       s(k,j)=ns(k,j)
2080    NEXT k
2090 NEXT j
2100 RETURN
2110 :
2120 :
2990 REM drawing procedure
3000 MOVE s(1,1),s(2,1)
3010 FOR i=2 TO n
3020    DRAW s(1,i),s(2,i)
3030 NEXT i
3040 DRAW s(1,1),s(2,1)
3050 RETURN
3060 :
3070 :
3990 REM x-rotation matrix procedure
4000 c(1,1)=1
4010 c(1,2)=0
4020 c(1,3)=0
4030 c(2,1)=0
4040 c(2,2)=COS(theta)
4050 c(2,3)=SIN(theta)
4060 c(3,1)=0
4070 c(3,2)=-SIN(theta)
4080 c(3,3)=COS(theta)
4090 RETURN
4100 :
4110 :
```

P51 Perspective

Most people will remember from school days about perspective. The method usually remembered is to locate a vanishing point. All parallel lines should converge to that point. We use a slight variation on this idea in this program.

In this routine we imagine that we have a fixed view point, the point (0,0,0) say, and we calculate the projection of the three dimensional object on an image plane, Z=K say. We will then have a two dimensional representation of the three dimensional object which will be in perspective.

Normally we do not wish to view from the point (0,0,0) and with an image plane at Z=K. We will normally have an arbitrary view point (VX,VY,VZ) and use the plane Z=0 as the image plane.

The algorithm to find the co-ordinates of an image point is then:

1. Rewrite the co-ordinates of the point with respect to the view point.
2. Calculate the co-ordinates of the projection in the plane Z=-VZ.
3. Rewrite the co-ordinates with respect to the old co-ordinates.
4. Draw the shape with the new co-ordinates.

This program uses the above routine to implement a perspective algorithm.

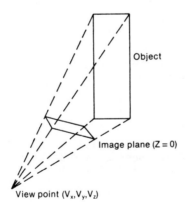

Object

Image plane (Z = 0)

View point (V$_x$,V$_y$,V$_z$)

COMMANDS

Key in the program and RUN.


```
100 REM Program - Perspective
110 MODE 1
120 PRINT:PRINT:PRINT
130 PRINT "This program shows a figure first of"
140 PRINT "all without considering perspective"
150 PRINT "then after the user requests, the"
160 PRINT "figure in perspective"
170 PRINT
180 PRINT "The figure chosen is a line drawing of"
190 PRINT "a house."
200 PRINT:PRINT:PRINT
210 PRINT "Press any key to continue"
220 z$=INKEY$:IF z$="" THEN 220
230 CLS
240 DIM h(10,3), s(10,3), p(10,3)
250 FOR i=1 TO 10
260   FOR j=1 TO 3
270     READ h(i,j):s(i,j)=h(i,j)
280   NEXT j
290 NEXT i
300 :
310 DATA 0,0,-200,100,0,-200,100,80,-200,50,100
320 DATA -200,0,80,-200,0,0,-50,100,0,-50,100
330 DATA 80,-50,50,100,-50,0,80,-50
340 :
350 MODE 2
360 ORIGIN 320,200
370 GOSUB 1000:REM draw house
380 :
390 r$="y"
400 WHILE r$="y" OR r$="Y"
410   :
415   LOCATE 1,24
420   INPUT "Viewpoint (x,y,z) ",vx,vy,vz
430   CLS
440   :
450   FOR i=1 TO 10
460     X=s(i,1):Y=s(i,2):Z=s(i,3)
470     GOSUB 2000:REM perspective calcs
480     p(i,1)=qx:p(i,2)=qy:p(i,3)=0
490   NEXT i
500   :
510   FOR i=1 TO 10
520     FOR j=1 TO 3
530       h(i,j)=p(i,j)
540     NEXT j
550   NEXT i
560   :
570   GOSUB 1000:REM draw house
580   LOCATE 1,25: PRINT "Another view?";
590   r$=INKEY$:IF r$="" THEN 590
600 WEND
610 END
```

```
990 REM Procedure to draw house
1000 MOVE h(1,1),h(1,2)
1010 FOR j=2 TO 5
1020    DRAW h(j,1),h(j,2)
1030 NEXT j
1040 DRAW h(1,1),h(1,2)
1050 REM next draw the back of the house
1060 MOVE h(6,1),h(6,2)
1070 FOR j=7 TO 10
1080    DRAW h(j,1),h(j,2)
1090 NEXT j
1100 DRAW h(6,1),h(6,2)
1110 REM join the back to the front
1120 MOVE h(6,1),h(6,2)
1130 DRAW h(1,1),h(1,2)
1140 MOVE h(10,1),h(10,2)
1150 DRAW h(5,1),h(5,2)
1160 MOVE h(9,1),h(9,2)
1170 DRAW h(4,1),h(4,2)
1180 MOVE h(8,1),h(8,2)
1190 DRAW h(3,1),h(3,2)
1200 MOVE h(7,1),h(7,2)
1210 DRAW h(2,1),h(2,2)
1220 RETURN
1230 :
1240 :
1990 REM Perspective calculations
2000 PX=X-vx
2010 PY=Y-vy
2020 PZ=Z-vz
2030 R=-vz/PZ
2040 qx=R*PX+vx
2050 qy=R*PY+vy
2060 RETURN
```

P52 Rotating House

Using the techniques developed in the previous programs, we
present here a program which shows an object continuously
rotating about the origin. The object chosen is a line
drawing of a house.

COMMANDS

Key in the program and RUN.


```
100 REM Program - Rotating house
110 MODE 1
120 PRINT:PRINT:PRINT
130 PRINT "This program shows a figure first of"
140 PRINT "all without considering perspective"
150 PRINT "then after the user requests, the"
160 PRINT "figure in perspective"
170 PRINT
180 PRINT "The figure chosen is a line drawing of"
190 PRINT "a house."
200 PRINT:PRINT:PRINT
210 PRINT "Press any key to continue"
220 z$=INKEY$:IF z$="" THEN 220
230 CLS
240 DIM h(10,3), s(10,3), p(10,3)
250 FOR i=1 TO 10
260    FOR j=1 TO 3
270      READ h(i,j):s(i,j)=h(i,j)
280    NEXT j
290 NEXT i
300 :
310 DATA 0,0,-200,100,0,-200,100,80,-200,50,100
320 DATA -200,0,80,-200,0,0,-50,100,0,-50,100
330 DATA 80,-50,50,100,-50,0,80,-50
340 :
350 MODE 2:BORDER 3
360 ORIGIN 320,200
370 GOSUB 640:REM draw house
380 vx=500:vy=500:vz=500:REM view point
390 GOSUB 1080:REM set up rotation array
400 :
410 WHILE 1=1
420    :
430    t=TIME
440    WHILE TIME<t+300:WEND
450    CLS
460    :
470    FOR i=1 TO 10
480      X=s(i,1):Y=s(i,2):Z=s(i,3)
490      GOSUB 900:REM perspective calcs
500      p(i,1)=qx:p(i,2)=qy:p(i,3)=0
```

```
510    NEXT i
520    :
530    FOR i=1 TO 10
540      FOR j=1 TO 3
550        h(i,j)=p(i,j)
560      NEXT j
570    NEXT i
580    :
590    GOSUB 640:REM draw house
600    GOSUB 980:REM rotate
610 WEND
620 END
630 REM Procedure to draw house
640 MOVE h(1,1),h(1,2)
650 FOR j=2 TO 5
660    DRAW h(j,1),h(j,2)
670 NEXT j
680 DRAW h(1,1),h(1,2)
690 REM next draw the back of the house
700 MOVE h(6,1),h(6,2)
710 FOR j=7 TO 10
720    DRAW h(j,1),h(j,2)
730 NEXT j
740 DRAW h(6,1),h(6,2)
750 REM join the back to the front
760 MOVE h(6,1),h(6,2)
770 DRAW h(1,1),h(1,2)
780 MOVE h(10,1),h(10,2)
790 DRAW h(5,1),h(5,2)
800 MOVE h(9,1),h(9,2)
810 DRAW h(4,1),h(4,2)
820 MOVE h(8,1),h(8,2)
830 DRAW h(3,1),h(3,2)
840 MOVE h(7,1),h(7,2)
850 DRAW h(2,1),h(2,2)
860 RETURN
870 :
880 :
890 REM Perspective calculations
900 PX=X-vx
910 PY=Y-vy
920 PZ=Z-vz
930 R=-vz/PZ
940 qx=R*PX+vx
950 qy=R*PY+vy
960 RETURN
970 REM Rotate procedure
980 FOR i=1 TO 10
990    a=c(1,1)*s(I,1)+c(2,1)*s(i,2)+c(3,1)*s(i,3)
1000   b=c(1,2)*s(I,1)+c(2,2)*s(i,2)+c(3,2)*s(i,3)
1010   c=c(1,3)*s(I,1)+c(2,3)*s(i,2)+c(3,3)*s(i,3)
1020   s(i,1)=a:s(i,2)=b:s(i,3)=c
1030 NEXT i
1040 RETURN
1050 :
1060 :
1070 REM rotation array
```

```
1080  c(1,1)=COS(PI/10)
1090  c(1,2)=0
1100  c(1,3)=-SIN(PI/10)
1110  c(2,1)=0
1120  c(2,2)=1
1130  c(2,3)=0
1140  c(3,1)=SIN(PI/10)
1150  c(3,2)=0
1160  c(3,3)=COS(PI/10)
1170  RETURN
1180  :
1190  :
```

P53 Doodle

This program allows the user to use the cursor control keys to doodle on the screen.

COMMANDS

Key in the program and RUN.
Follow instructions.

```
100 REM Program - Doodle
110 MODE 0
120 ORIGIN 320,200
125 c=1
130 WHILE 1=1
140   dx=(INKEY(8)=0)-(INKEY(1)=0)
150   dy=(INKEY(2)=0)-(INKEY(0)=0)
170   DRAWR dx,dy
180 WEND
```

P54 Graph

This program shows how a 3 dimensional view of a surface defined mathematically can be drawn. The user has the choice of using hidden line removal or not. The surface takes a little time to draw, this could of course be speeded up. Change the code if you wish to try other surfaces.

COMMANDS

Key in program and RUN.
Follow instructions.


```
100 REM Program - 3D Graph Plot
110 MODE 2
120 DIM upper(640),lower(640)
130 INPUT "Hidden line (Y/N)",ans$
140 IF LEFT$(ans$,1)="Y" THEN lne=-1 ELSE lne=0
150 centx=320:centy=200
160 viewx=275:viewz=120
170 REM curve parms
180 ht=40:ohm=0.043
190 :
200 FOR i=1 TO 640
210   upper(i)=0
220   lower(i)=1000
230 NEXT i
240 :
250 FOR z=viewz-1 TO -viewz+1 STEP -5
260   lowx=INT(viewx*SQR(1-z*z/viewz/viewz)+0.5)
270   x=-lowx
280   y=ht*SIN(ohm*SQR(x*x+z*z))
290   x1=x+centx+z
300   y1=INT(400-(centy+y+z/2)+0.5)
310   FOR x=-lowx+1 TO lowx-1
320     y=ht*SIN(ohm*SQR(x*x + z*z))
330     x2=centx+x+z
340     y2=INT(400-(centy+y+z/2)+0.5)
350     IF lne=0 THEN GOTO 390
360     IF y2<lower(x2) THEN GOSUB 460
370     IF y2>upper(x2)
            THEN upper(x2)=y2:MOVE x1,y1:DRAW x2,y2
380     GOTO 400
390     MOVE x1,y1:DRAW x2,y2
400     x1=x2
410     y1=y2
420   NEXT x
430 NEXT z
440 END
450 :
460 lower(x2)=y2
470 IF upper(x2)=0 THEN upper(x2)=y2
480 RETURN
```

P55   3D Bar Chart

This program shows how a 3 dimensional bar chart can be drawn using the features of the Amstrad.

COMMANDS

Key in program and RUN.
Follow instructions.


```
100 REM Program 3D Bar Chart
110 MODE 0
120 k1=5:k2=20:k3=10
130 REM draw background
140 p=100:q=100
150 MOVE p,q:DRAWR 300,300*k1/k3,1:
              DRAWR 200,-200*k1/k2,1
160 DRAWR -300,-300*k1/k3,1:DRAWR -200,200*k1/k2,1
170 FOR i=1 TO 3
180    MOVE p,i*50+q:DRAWR 300,300*k1/k3,1:
              DRAWR 200,-200*k1/k2,1
190 NEXT i
200 MOVE p,q:DRAWR 0,150,1
210 MOVER 300,300*k1/k3:DRAWR 0,-150,1
220 MOVER 200,-200*k1/k2:DRAWR 0,150,1
230 :
240 REM place back bars
250 ik=2:off=80
260 READ h:x=p+40:y=q-8:GOSUB 450
270 FOR j=1 TO 3
280 READ h:x=x+off:y=y+off*k1/k3:GOSUB 450
290 NEXT j
300 REM place next row
310 ik=3:off=80
320 READ h:x=p+190:y=q-20:GOSUB 450
330 FOR j=1 TO 3
340 READ h:x=x+off:y=y+off*k1/k3:GOSUB 450
350 NEXT j
360 REM row 3
370 ik=4:off=80
380 READ h:x=p+240:y=q-32:GOSUB 450
390 FOR j=1 TO 3
400 READ h:x=x+off:y=y+off*k1/k3:GOSUB 450
410 NEXT j
420 :
430 z$=INKEY$:IF z$="" THEN 430
440 END
450 REM MOVE x,y:DRAWR 0,h,ik
460 FOR p=0 TO k2 STEP 2
470    MOVE p+x,y-p*k1/k2
480    DRAWR 0,h,ik
490    DRAWR k3,k1,ik
```

```
500 NEXT p
510 :
520 FOR p=k3 TO 0 STEP -2
530    MOVE x+k2+p,y-(k3-p)*k1/k3
540    DRAWR 0,h,ik
550 NEXT p
560 :
570 MOVE x+k2,y-k3*k1/k3
580 DRAWR 0,h+2,0
590 DRAWR k3,k1,0
600 MOVE x,y+h:DRAWR k2,-k1,0
610 RETURN
620 DATA 100,80,120,100,150,60,100
630 DATA 100,140,75,126,150
```

P56 Bar Chart

This program can draw a chart of up to thirty bars on to the
screen. The bars are automatically scaled to fit onto the
screen. The chart is not labelled. This is left as an
exercise for the reader.

COMMANDS

Key in the program and RUN.
Enter the number of bars, less than 30.
Enter the value of each bar as requested.


```
100 REM Program - BAR CHART
110 MODE 1
120 SYMBOL 244,126,126,126,126,126,126,126,126
130 SYMBOL 245,24,24,24,24,24,24,24,24
140 SYMBOL 246,0,0,0,0,0,0,0,255
150 DEF FNprt$(a)=RIGHT$("    "+STR$(a),3)
160 INPUT "Enter number of bars (<30) ",bars
170 DIM value(bars)
180 maximum=0
190 FOR i=1 TO bars
200    LOCATE 1,5
210    INPUT "Value of bar ",value(i)
220    IF value(i)>maximum THEN maximum=value(i)
230 NEXT i
240 :
250 CLS
260 scale=1
270 IF maximum>20 THEN scale=maximum/20
280 :
290 FOR i=1 TO bars
300    value(i)=INT(value(i)/scale)
310 NEXT i
320 :
330 FOR i=1 TO 20 STEP 2
340    LOCATE 1,22-i:PRINT FNprt$(INT(i*scale))
350 NEXT i
360 :
370 FOR i=1 TO 23
380    LOCATE 4,i:PRINT CHR$(245);
390 NEXT i
400 :
410 FOR i=1 TO bars+4
420    LOCATE 4+i,22:PRINT CHR$(246);
430 NEXT i
440 :
450 FOR i=1 TO bars
460    FOR j=1 TO value(i)
470       LOCATE 7+i,22-j:PRINT CHR$(244);
```

```
480    NEXT j
490 NEXT i
500 z$=INKEY$:IF z$="" THEN 500
```

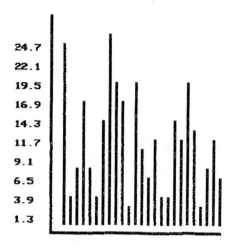

P57 Pie Chart

This is a fairly self explanatory program which can be used to produce a pie chart on screen.

To speed up the initial display of the chart, we have included a parameter to indicate the resolution of the pie chart. If the resolution is coarse, 0.2, say, the resulting chart may not be very accurate. So if you are generally happy, with the chart, then you could redraw the chart with a finer resolution for your final copy.

COMMANDS

Key in the program and RUN.
Enter data when requested.


```
100 REM Program - PIE Chart
110 DIM item(20)
120 MODE 1
130 :
140 PRINT "This program depicts a PIE chart based"
150 PRINT "on data which you enter, one at a time"
160 PRINT "Different areas of the pie chart are"
170 PRINT "painted in different colours, thus we"
180 PRINT "will plot the data in mode 0"
190 PRINT:PRINT:
200 PRINT "Enter tha data one item at a time."
210 PRINT "Enter 0 to finish."
220 i=0:total=0
230 item(i)=1:REM this item is not used
240 WHILE item(i)<>0 AND i<20
250    i=i+1
260    LOCATE 5,15:PRINT "Enter item -";SPACE$(20);
270    LOCATE 19,15:INPUT "",item(i)
280    total=total+item(i)
290 WEND
300 IF i<20 THEN GOTO 360
310 PRINT "We have run out of room for data"
320 PRINT "Do you wish to proceed with plotting?"
330 z$=INKEY$:IF z$="" THEN 330
340 IF z$="n" OR z$="N" THEN STOP
350 INPUT "Resolution in radians ",res
360 INPUT "Resolution in radians ",res
370 repeat=-1:CLS
380 WHILE repeat
390    CLS
400    PRINT SPACE$(15);"PIE CHART"
410    IF (i-1) MOD 3=1 THEN flag=-1 ELSE flag=0
```

```
420    IF flag=-1 THEN last.item=i-2 ELSE last.item=i-1
430    last.angle=0:angle=0
440    ORIGIN 320,200
450    :
460    FOR j=1 TO last.item
470      c=(j MOD 3)+1
480      GOSUB 590:REM draw segment
490      last.angle=last.angle + 2*PI*item(j)/total
500    NEXT j
510    :
520    IF flag=-1 THEN c=3:GOSUB 590
530    LOCATE 1,24:PRINT "New resolution";
540    z$=INKEY$:IF z$="" THEN 540
550    IF z$="Y" OR z$="y" THEN PRINT:
       INPUT "Resolution ",res ELSE repeat=0
560 WEND
570 END
580 REM Routine to draw segment
590 WHILE angle<last.angle+2*PI*item(j)/total
600    MOVE 0,0
610    DRAW 120*COS(angle),120*SIN(angle),c
620    angle=angle+res
630 WEND
640 RETURN
```

P58 Mean and Standard Deviation

This program is used to find the mean and standard deviation of a list of data items.

COMMANDS

Key in the program and RUN.
Follow instructions.

```
100 REM Program - Mean and Standard Deviation
110 MODE 1
120 fin=0:flag=0:mean=0:dev=0:total=0
130 nos=0:sums=0:a$=""
140 PRINT:PRINT
150 PRINT "This program can be used to calculate"
160 PRINT "the mean and standard deviation of a "
170 PRINT "set of numeric data.  The data is "
180 PRINT "entered one item at a time, terminated"
190 PRINT "by a non-numeric item."
200 PRINT:PRINT
210 :
220 WHILE fin=0
230    LOCATE 10,20:PRINT "Next item ";SPACE$(16);
240    k=0
250    REM get first character
260    b$=INKEY$:IF b$="" THEN 260
270    IF b$="." THEN k=k+1
280    b=(VAL(b$)=0) AND
          NOT(b$="0" OR b$="." OR b$="-" OR b$="+")
290    IF b THEN fin=-1: GOTO 510
300    LOCATE 25,20:PRINT b$
310    a$=b$
320    FOR i=1 TO 14
330       b=(1=1)
340       WHILE b
350          b$=INKEY$:IF b$="" THEN 350
360          IF b$="." THEN k=k+1:b=0:GOTO 390
370          b=(VAL(b$)=0) AND
                NOT(b$="0" OR b$="." OR ASC(b$)=13)
380          IF b THEN PRINT CHR$(7);
390          IF k>1 THEN PRINT CHR$(7);
400       WEND
410       :
420       IF ASC(b$)=13 THEN i=14:flag=1 ELSE a$=a$+b$
430       LOCATE 25+i,20:PRINT b$
440    NEXT i
450    :
460    a=VAL(a$)
470    total=total+a
480    nos=nos+1
```

```
490    sums=sums+a*a
500    numb$=a$+","+numb$
510 WEND
520 :
530 CLS
540 mean=total/nos
550 dev=SQR(sums/nos - mean*mean)
560 PRINT "The mean of the data is "mean
570 PRINT:PRINT:PRINT
580 PRINT "The standard deviation is "dev
590 PRINT:PRINT:PRINT
600 PRINT "The data were - "
610 PRINT numb$
620 END
```

P59 Bubble Sort

This program is demonstration of how the classical Bubble Sort works. The program sorts ten numbers on the screen.

COMMANDS

Key in the program and RUN.
Follow instructions.


```
100 REM Program - Bubble Sort
110 DIM nos%(10)
120 MODE 0
130 n=10
140 BORDER 1:PEN 7:PAPER 12:CLS
150 PRINT "How many digits does";
160 PRINT "each number have";
170 INPUT d
180 PRINT "Enter 10 numbers"
190 :
200 FOR i=1 TO n
210    INPUT nos%(i)
220    IF LEN(STR$(nos%(i)))<>d+1 THEN
          PRINT CHR$(7):i=i-1
230 NEXT i
240 :
250 INPUT "Speed of processing (1 to 10)",sped
260 sped=sped*50
270 :
280 CLS
290 REM print array onto screen
300 FOR i=1 TO 10
310    LOCATE 5,i*2:PRINT nos%(i);
320 NEXT i
330 :
340 LOCATE 1,25:PRINT "Press any key";
350 z$=INKEY$:IF z$="" THEN 350
360 LOCATE 1,25:PRINT SPACE$(13);
370 :
380 REM Sort routine
390 :
400 FOR i=1 TO n-1
410    FOR j=i+1 TO n
420       PEN 3
430       GOSUB 530
440       FOR k=1 TO sped:NEXT k
450       IF nos%(j)>nos%(i) THEN GOSUB 580
460       PEN 7
470       GOSUB 530
480    NEXT j
490 NEXT i
500 END
```

```
510 :
520 REM Routine to colour two items
530 LOCATE 5,i*2:PRINT nos%(i);
540 LOCATE 5,j*2:PRINT nos%(j);
550 RETURN
560 :
570 REM routine to swap two items
580 PEN 1
590 GOSUB 530
600 FOR k=1 TO sped:NEXT k
610 t%=nos%(j)
620 nos%(j)=nos%(i)
630 nos%(i)=t%
640 FOR k=1 TO sped:NEXT k
650 PEN 7
660 GOSUB 530
670 PRINT CHR$(7);
680 RETURN
```

P60   Shell Sort

This is the classical fast Shell Sort routine. As with the
Bubble sort, the sorting is carried out on the screen. It
can be a very useful exercise to try and figure out why the
Shell routine works.

COMMANDS

Key in the program and RUN.
Follow instructions


```
100 REM Program - Shell Sort
110 DIM nos%(9)
120 MODE 0
130 n=10
140 BORDER 1:PEN 7:PAPER 12:CLS
150 PRINT "How many digits does";
160 PRINT "each number have";
170 INPUT d
180 PRINT "Enter 10 numbers"
190 :
200 FOR i=0 TO n-1
210    INPUT nos%(i)
220    IF LEN(STR$(nos%(i)))<>d+1 THEN PRINT CHR$(7):i=i-1
230 NEXT i
240 :
250 INPUT "Speed of processing (1 to 10)",sped
260 sped=sped*50
270 :
280 CLS
290 REM print array onto screen
300 FOR i=0 TO 9
310    LOCATE 5,(i+1)*2:PRINT nos%(i);
320 NEXT i
330 :
340 LOCATE 1,25:PRINT "Press any key";
350 z$=INKEY$:IF z$="" THEN 350
360 LOCATE 1,25:PRINT SPACE$(13);
370 :
380 REM Sort routine
390 :
400 dist%=(n-1)/2
410 WHILE dist%>0
420    FOR i=dist%+1 TO n-1
430      FOR j=i-dist% TO 0 STEP -dist%
440        point=j+dist%
450        PEN 3:GOSUB 570
460        FOR k=1 TO sped:NEXT k
470        IF nos%(j)>nos%(point) THEN GOSUB 620
480        PEN 7:GOSUB 570
490      NEXT j
```

```
500    NEXT i
510    dist%=INT(dist%/2)
520 WEND
530 LOCATE 1,25
540 END
550 :
560 REM Routine to colour two items
570 LOCATE 5,(point+1)*2:PRINT nos%(point);
580 LOCATE 5,(j+1)*2:PRINT nos%(j);
590 RETURN
600 :
610 REM routine to swap two items
620 PEN 1
630 GOSUB 570
640 FOR k=1 TO sped:NEXT k
650 t%=nos%(j)
660 nos%(j)=nos%(point)
670 nos%(point)=t%
680 FOR k=1 TO sped:NEXT k
690 PEN 7
700 GOSUB 570
710 PRINT CHR$(7);
720 RETURN
```

P61 Merge

A common need in data processing is the ability to merge two sorted files to produce a third sorted file.

It is quicker to sort small files and then to merge the files to form larger ones. In this program, we mimic file handling by using arrays. The array elements are entered via the keyboard but the program could be amended to allow the elements to be entered via tape files.

COMMANDS

Key in the program and RUN.
Enter the array elements when prompted in increasing order.

```
100 REM Program - Merge
110 MODE 1
120 PRINT "This program is used to merge two "
130 PRINT "arrays of data.Each array can hold up"
140 PRINT "to 100 data items.  This program would"
150 PRINT "beused with a disk based sort routine."
160 PRINT "Each array must be entered in increasing order."
170 PRINT:PRINT:PRINT
180 DIM array1(100),array2(100),mrge(100)
190 :
200 i=0:array1(i)=1
210 WHILE i<101 AND array1(i)<>0
220     i=i+1
230     LOCATE 1,10:PRINT SPACE$(40);
240     LOCATE 1,10:INPUT "Array1 element (0 to finish)",
                      array1(i)
250     IF NOT(array1(i)<>0 AND array1(i-1)>array1(i)) THEN 300
260     LOCATE 1,10:PRINT "OUT OF ORDER................";
270     i=i-1
280     PRINT CHR$(7);CHR$(7);
290     FOR k=1 TO 500:NEXT k
300 WEND
310 n1=i-1
320 :
330 i=0:array2(i)=1
340 WHILE i<101 AND array2(i)<>0
350     i=i+1
360     LOCATE 1,12:PRINT SPACE$(40);
370     LOCATE 1,12:INPUT "Array2 element (0 to finish)",
                      array2(i)
380     IF NOT(array2(i)<>0 AND array2(i-1)>array2(i)) THEN 430
390     LOCATE 1,12:PRINT "OUT OF ORDER................";
400     i=i-1
410     PRINT CHR$(7);CHR$(7);
420     FOR k=1 TO 500:NEXT k
430 WEND
440 n2=i-1
```

```
450 :
460 i=1:j=1
470 WHILE NOT(array1(i)=0 OR array2(j)=0)
480     IF array1(i)<array2(j)
            THEN mrge(i+j-1)=array1(i):i=i+1
            ELSE mrge(i+j-1)=array2(j):j=j+1
490 WEND
500 :
510 IF array1(i)=0 THEN 580
520 :
530 FOR k=i TO n1
540   mrge(k+j-1)=array1(k)
550 NEXT k
560 GOTO 620
570 :
580 FOR k=j TO n2
590   mrge(k+i-1)=array2(k)
600 NEXT k
610 :
620 CLS
630 PRINT "Array 1 consisted of :"
640 FOR i=1 TO n1
650   PRINT array1(i)
660 NEXT i
670 :
680 PRINT "Array 2 consisted of :"
690 FOR i=1 TO n2
700   PRINT array2(i)
710 NEXT i
720 PRINT "The merged array is :"
730 FOR i=1 TO n1+n2
740   PRINT mrge(i)
750 NEXT i
760 :
770 END
```

P62 Binary Search

If you have a mass of data sorted into order, then it is very inefficient to search for a particular item in a sequential manner. For instance, when looking for a word in a dictionary, you would not consider every word in sequence until you found the required entry.

A more efficient search method is to open the dictionary in the middle and decide which half of the book the word is in. You then take this half of the book and half it again. This routine is repeated until the page holding your word is found.

This program performs a similar search on a set of data – a price list.

COMMANDS

Key in the program and RUN.
Enter item from price list.

```
100 REM Program - Binary Search
110 DIM item$(100),price(100)
120 MODE 1
130 PRINT : PRINT : PRINT
140 PRINT "This program shows how the computer"
150 PRINT "can be used to quickly look up a set of "
160 PRINT "data. We assume that the data have been"
170 PRINT "sorted into alphabetic order, for the"
180 PRINT "purposes of this program the data are"
190 PRINT "held in data statements. In this case"
200 PRINT "the data constitute a price list."
210 PRINT:PRINT
220 PRINT "Press any key to continue"
230 z$=INKEY$:IF z$="" THEN 230
240 CLS
250 i=0:item$(i)="s"
260 WHILE item$(i)<>"zzz"
270     i=i+1
280     READ item$(i),price(i)
290 WEND
300 :
310 n%=i-1
320 res$="Y"
330 WHILE LEFT$(res$,1)="Y" OR LEFT$(res$,1)="y"
340     INPUT "Which item do you require"; item$
350     item$=UPPER$(item$)
360     m%=n%\2
370     el%=m%
380     found=0
390     there=0
```

```
400     WHILE NOT(found) AND NOT(there)
410        IF item$<item$(m%+1) AND item$>item$(m%-1) AND
              NOT found THEN there=-1
420        IF item$=item$(m%) THEN found=-1
430        IF item$<item$(m%) THEN el%=el%\2:m%=m%-el%+(el%=0)
440        IF item$>item$(m%) THEN el%=el%\2:m%=m%+el%-(el%=0)
450        WHILE m%>n%
460          el%=el%\2
470          m%=m%-el%+(el%=0)
480        WEND
490     WEND
500     :
510     IF found THEN PRINT:PRINT:PRINT item$(m%),price(m%)
                   ELSE PRINT:PRINT:PRINT "Item not in list"
520     INPUT "Another ",res$
530 WEND
540 END
550 :
560 DATA APPLES,30.1,BAG,12.09,BAG-BLUE,56.34,BANANA,3.10,
         BANGER,123.32,BEER-EXPORT,0.45,BEER-LAGER,0.55
570 DATA BEER-STOUT,0.67,BOOZE,4.34,BOTTLE,90.2,
         BOTTLE-GREEN,3.45,BOVRIL,0.75
580 DATA CABBAGE,0.76,CANADA DRY,0.78,CANADIAN CLUB,7.35,
         CARROTS,0.30,COD LIVER OIL,0.76,COMPUTERS,299.99
590 DATA COOKERS,0.65,CRAB-APPLES,0.00
600 DATA DIGGERS,4567.34,DISC DRIVES,250.67,DISCS DDDS,2.55,
         DISCS SDSS,1.80,DOZERS,123456.78
610 DATA EMPIRE BISCUITS,.70,EMULATOR,6577,ENAMEL-RED,7.35,
         ENAMEL-WHITE,8.35,ENGINE-CAR,50.56,ENGINE-SCOOTER,45.76,
         FAN,5.79,FARM,1000000
620 DATA zzz,0
```

P63 Permutations

This program can be used to find the number of permutations of n objects taken r at a time. This is a very useful routine in statistics.

COMMANDS

Key in the program and RUN.
Follow instructions.

```
100 REM Program - Permutations
110 MODE 1
120 PRINT:PRINT
130 PRINT "This program can be used to find the"
140 PRINT "number of permutations of n objects"
150 PRINT "taken r at a time."
160 PRINT
170 PRINT "For example, suppose there are 4 people"
180 PRINT "in a race, then how many ways can the"
190 PRINT "first 3 positions be filled?"
200 PRINT:PRINT
210 PRINT "Suppose the racers are called A,B,C & D"
220 PRINT "then possible finishing positions"
230 PRINT "would be :"
240 PRINT
250 PRINT "ABC BAC BCA CAB CBA ACB"
260 PRINT "ABD ADB BDA BAD DBA DAB"
270 PRINT "ACD ADC CAD CDA DAC DCA"
280 PRINT "BCD BDC CBD CDB DBC DCB"
290 PRINT
300 PRINT "In this example there are 24 ways of"
310 PRINT "placing the first 3 in the race."
320 PRINT:PRINT
330 PRINT "Press any key to continue"
340 z$=INKEY$:IF z$="" THEN 340
350 CLS
360 PRINT "This program will allow the user to"
370 PRINT "calculate the number of permutations"
380 PRINT:PRINT:PRINT
390 INPUT "Number of objects ",n
400 INPUT "Value of r - size of the group ",r
410 k=n:GOSUB 480:num=m
420 k=n-r:GOSUB 480:den=m
430 perms=num/den
440 PRINT:PRINT:PRINT
450 PRINT "Number of permutations = ";perms
460 END
470 REM factorial subroutine
480 m=1
```

```
490 FOR i=1 TO k
500    m=m*i
510 NEXT i
520 RETURN
```

P64 Combinations

This program finds the number of combinations of n objects taken r at a time.

COMMANDS

Key in the program and RUN.
Follow instructions.

```
100 REM Program - Combinations
110 MODE 1
120 PRINT:PRINT
130 PRINT "This program can be used to find the"
140 PRINT "number of combinations of n objects"
150 PRINT "taken r at a time."
160 PRINT
170 PRINT "For example, suppose we wish to make up"
180 PRINT "a committee of 3 people out of a pool"
190 PRINT "of 4 people. How many ways can this "
200 PRINT "be done?"
210 PRINT:PRINT
220 PRINT "Suppose the people are called A,B,C & D"
230 PRINT "Then possible combinations would be:"
240 PRINT
250 PRINT "ABC ABD ACD BCD"
260 PRINT
270 PRINT "In this example there are 4 ways of"
280 PRINT "making up the committee."
290 PRINT:PRINT
300 PRINT "Press any key to continue"
310 z$=INKEY$:IF z$="" THEN 310
320 CLS
330 PRINT "This program will allow the user to"
340 PRINT "calculate the number of combinations"
350 PRINT:PRINT:PRINT
360 INPUT "Number of objects ",n
370 INPUT "Value of r - size of the group ",r
380 k=n:GOSUB 470:num=m
390 k=n-r:GOSUB 470:den=m
400 num=num/den
410 k=r:GOSUB 470:den=m
420 perms=num/den
430 PRINT:PRINT:PRINT
440 PRINT "Number of permutations = ";perms
450 END
460 REM factorial subroutine
470 m=1
480 FOR i=1 TO k
490    m=m*i
500 NEXT i
510 RETURN
```

P65 Least Squares

This program uses the method of least squares to find the
best straight line through a set of data points.

The straight line found is in the form

        Y=MX+B

when the equation is formed it is printed out.

COMMANDS

Key in the program and RUN.
Enter the data items in the form X,Y.


```
100 REM Program - Least Squares
110 MODE 1
120 LOCATE 13,4:PRINT "LEAST SQUARES"
130 PRINT:PRINT:PRINT
140 INPUT "How many data points ",n
150 PRINT:PRINT:PRINT
160 DIM x(n),y(n)
170 FOR i=1 TO n
180     INPUT; "X=",x(i):INPUT "  Y=",y(i)
190     sum.x=sum.x+x(i)
200     sum.x.sq=sum.x.sq+x(i)*x(i)
210     sum.y=sum.y+y(i)
220     sum.xy=sum.xy + x(i)*y(i)
230 NEXT i
240 :
250 d=n*sum.x.sq - sum.x*sum.x
260 IF d=0 THEN PRINT "NO FIT POSSIBLE !!!":END
270 :
280 m=(n*sum.xy - sum.x*sum.y)/d
290 b=sum.y/n - m*sum.x/n
300 :
310 max.x=x(1):min.x=x(1)
320 max.y=y(1):min.y=y(1)
330 FOR i=2 TO n
340     max.x=MAX(max.x,x(i))
350     min.x=MIN(min.x,x(i))
360     max.y=MAX(max.y,y(i))
370     min.y=MIN(min.y,y(i))
380 NEXT i
390 :
400 MODE 2
410 IF min.x>0 THEN min.x=0
420 IF min.y>0 THEN min.y=0
430 range.x=max.x-min.x
440 range.y=max.x-min.y
450 REM plot will not work for all negative data
```

```
460 scale.x=640/range.x
470 scale.y=400/range.y
480 ORIGIN ABS(min.x*scale.x),ABS(min.y*scale.y)
490 MOVE min.x*scale.x,0:DRAW max.x*scale.x,0
500 MOVE 0,min.y*scale.y:DRAW 0,max.y*scale.y
510 :
520 FOR i=1 TO n
530   MOVE x(i)*scale.x,y(i)*scale.y-5
540   DRAWR 0,10:MOVER -5,-5:DRAWR 10,y
550 NEXT i
560 :
570 MOVE min.x*scale.x,(m*min.x + b)*scale.y
580 DRAW max.x*scale.x,(m*max.x + b)*scale.y
590 LOCATE 1,1:PRINT "Line is Y="m"*X+"b
600 END
```

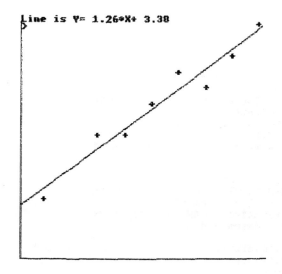

P66　File Dump Utility

This program can be used to dump a file on disk　or　tape　to either the screen or to a printer. It is very useful to check that a data file has been set up correctly.

Note that BASIC　program　files　cannot　be　dumped　by　this method.

COMMANDS

Key in program and RUN.
Follow the instructions.


```
10 REM File dump
20 INK 0,1
30 INK 1,24
40 PAPER 0
50 PEN 1
60 BORDER 1
70 MODE 1
80 PRINT TAB(17)"FILE DUMP"
90 PRINT TAB(17)"---------"
100 PRINT:PRINT
110 PRINT"This program dumps a sequential file to"
120 PRINT"the screen or to a printer."
130 PRINT
140 PRINT"Note that a normal BASIC  program  file"
150 PRINT"cannot be dumped by this method."
160 PRINT
170 PRINT"Press key 1 or 2 to select:"
180 PRINT
190 PRINT TAB(8)"1 - Screen"
200 PRINT TAB(8)"2 - Printer"
210 a$=INKEY$:IF a$<>"1" AND a$<>"2" THEN 210
220 IF a$="2" THEN device=8
230 PRINT:PRINT
240 PRINT"Insert the tape or disk  containing the"
250 PRINT"file."
260 PRINT
270 INPUT"What is the name of the file";fl$
280 IF LEN(fl$)>8 THEN fl$=LEFT$(fl$,8)
290 :
300 CLS
310 OPENIN fl$
320 DIM item$(500)
330 REM Above line defines maximum file size.
340 WHILE EOF=0 AND n<501
350 : INPUT #9,item$(n)
360 : n=n+1
370 WEND
```

```
380 CLOSEIN
390 PRINT
400 PRINT"File has been read.  Press any key."
410 a$=INKEY$:IF a$="" THEN 410
420 :
430 MODE 2
440 FOR k=0 TO n
450 :   PRINT #device,item$(k)
460 :   IF device=0 THEN c=c+1
470 :   IF c=20 THEN GOSUB 610
480 NEXT
490 :
500 PRINT
510 PRINT"End of file - Press any key."
520 a$=INKEY$:IF a$="" THEN 520
530 CLS
540 INPUT"Another file (y/n)";y$
550 IF LEFT$(LOWER$(y$),1)="y" THEN RUN
560 MODE 1
570 END
580 :
590 :
600 REM Screen full
610 PRINT
620 PRINT"Press any key to continue."
630 a$=INKEY$:IF a$="" THEN 630
640 c=0
650 CLS
660 RETURN
```

P67 Exercise Class

This program could help you keep fit. See if you can keep in time with the exercise class.

CAUTION - This is not recommended for those with heart trouble.

COMMANDS

Key in the program and RUN.


```
10 REM Exercise class
20 BORDER 2
30 PAPER 0
40 INK 0,26
50 MODE 0
60 s$=SPACE$(3)
70 :
80 FOR n=0 TO 11
90 : INK n+1,n
100 NEXT
110 :
120 WHILE LEN(a$)=0
130 :   FOR ch=248 TO 251
140 :     LOCATE 1,8
150 :       FOR n=1 TO 12 STEP 4
160 :         FOR k=0 TO 3
170 :           PEN n+k
180 :           PRINT s$;CHR$(ch);
190 :         NEXT
200 :         PRINT:PRINT:PRINT
210 :       NEXT
220 :     c%=30+50*RND(1)
230 :     h%=(252-ch)*20+c%
240 :     SOUND 81,h%,20,5
250 :     SOUND 74,h%/3,20,5
260 :     RELEASE 3
270 :   NEXT
280 :   a$=INKEY$
290 WEND
300 :
310 PEN 1
320 MODE 1
330 END
```

P68 Biorhythms

It has been said that a human being has predictable ups and downs. The proponents of biorhythms state that there are three main cycles in life - the Physical, Emotional and Intellectual.

This program is used to show the biorhythms for any particular person at any point in his life. The program displays the three biorhythms for approximately a month from the date of interest.

COMMANDS

Key in the program and RUN.
Follow instructions.
Interpret biorhythms.


```
100 REM Program - BIORHYTHMS
110 DEFINT d,m,y
120 CLS
130 PRINT : PRINT
140 PRINT "This progam displays the BIORHYTHMS"
150 PRINT "of a subject for any range of days"
160 PRINT:PRINT:PRINT
170 PRINT "The program uses the Gregorian calendar"
180 PRINT : PRINT : PRINT
190 PRINT "Enter date of interest"
200 d1=0:m1=0:y1=0
210 WHILE d1<1 OR d1>31
220    INPUT "Day (1-31)"; d1
230 WEND
240 WHILE m1<1 OR m1>12
250    INPUT "Month (1-12)";m1
260 WEND
270 WHILE y1<1
280    INPUT "Year (eg 1985)";y1
290 WEND
300 dd=d1:mm=m1:yy=y1:GOSUB 720
310 n1=nn
320 :
330 PRINT : PRINT "Enter date of birth of subject"
340 d2=0:m2=0:y2=0
350 WHILE d2<1 OR d2>31
360    INPUT "Day (1-31)"; d2
370 WEND
380 WHILE m2<1 OR m2>12
390    INPUT "Month (1-12)";m2
400 WEND
410 WHILE y2<1
420    INPUT "Year (eg 1985)";y2
430 WEND
```

```
440 dd=d2:mm=m2:yy=y2:GOSUB 720
450 n2=nn
460 daysalive=n1-n2
470 IF daysalive<1 THEN PRINT:PRINT "Don't be silly":STOP
480 PRINT
490 PRINT "At the date of interest, the subject"
500 PRINT "had lived ";daysalive;" days."
510 PRINT "Press any key to continue";
520 z$=INKEY$:IF z$="" THEN 520
530 :
540 MODE 1
550 MOVE 0,200: DRAW 639,200,3
560 FOR d=1 TO 31
570    MOVE d*20,210:DRAW d*20,190
580 NEXT d
590 :
600 PEN 1: PRINT "Physical"
610 p=23:c=1:GOSUB 860
620 PEN 2: PRINT "Emotional"
630 p=28:c=2:GOSUB 860
640 PEN 3: PRINT "Intellectual"
650 p=33:c=3:GOSUB 860
660 :
670 FOR i=1 TO 6:PRINT :NEXT i
680 PRINT "T":PRINT "o":PRINT "d":PRINT "a":PRINT "y"
690 GOTO 690
700 :
710 :
720 REM Subroutine to calculate no of
730 REM days since day zero
740 REM
750 REM INPUTS : dd,mm,yy
760 REM OUTPUT - nn
770 RESTORE
780 FOR i=1 TO mm
790    READ dty
800 NEXT i
810 DATA 0,31,59,90,120,151,181,212,243,273,304,334
820 dty=dty + dd
830 nn=dty + yy*365 + INT(yy/4) +1 - INT(yy/100) + INT(yy/400)
840 IF (yy MOD 4 =0) AND mm<3 THEN nn=nn-1
850 RETURN
860 REM Plotting subroutine
870 REM
880 REM This draws out each bio
890 REM INPUTS - p and c
900 MOVE 0,INT(200*SIN(2*PI*(daysalive)/p)+200)
910 FOR x=0 TO 640 STEP 2
920    y=INT(200*SIN(2*PI*(daysalive + x/20)/p)+200)
930    DRAW x,y,c
940 NEXT x
950 RETURN
```

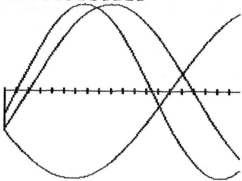

P69   Wheel of Fortune

This program can prove to be a very useful aid in fund raising. The effect of the wheel is better when using a large video screen.

COMMANDS

Key in the program and RUN.


```
100 REM WHEEL OF FORTUNE
110 MODE 1
120 BORDER 9
130 INK 0,21:INK 1,8
140 PEN 1
150 LOCATE 5,5:PRINT "GOOD EVENING friends and"
160 LOCATE 5,6:PRINT "WELCOME to the CPC 464"
170 PEN 3
180 LOCATE 5,8:PRINT "  WHEEL OF FORTUNE"
190 PEN 1
200 LOCATE 5,10:PRINT "Why don't you step up and"
210 LOCATE 5,11:PRINT "try your luck? Pick a "
220 LOCATE 5,12:PRINT "number between 1 and 30"
230 LOCATE 5,13:PRINT "and gamble away"
240 PEN 2
250 LOCATE 5,20:PRINT "PRESS ANY KEY TO CONTINUE"
260 A$=INKEY$:IF A$="" THEN 260
270 REM DRAW WHEEL OF FORTUNE
280 :
290 MODE 2
300 ORIGIN 320,199
310 FOR I=1 TO 30
320    MOVE 0,0
330    K=2*PI/30*I
340    DRAW 150*COS(K),150*SIN(K)
350 NEXT I
360 PEN 1
370 FOR N=0 TO 29
380    K=(2*N+1)/30*PI
390    LOCATE (155*COS(K)+320)/8,25-(155*SIN(K)+199)/16
400    PRINT N+1;
410 NEXT N
420 :
430 LOCATE 1,25:PRINT "PRESS ANY KEY TO START";
440 A$=INKEY$:IF A$="" THEN 440
450 LOCATE 1,25:PRINT "                        ";
460 REM GET TIME TO SPIN WHEEL
470 T=TIME
480 T1=(INT(RND(2)*20))*300+100
490 EVERY 15,1 GOSUB 660
500 p=10
510 WHILE TIME<T+T1
520    A=(TIME-T)/600*PI
```

```
530    MOVE 0,0
540    PRINT CHR$(23)+CHR$(1);
550    DRAW 150*COS(A),150*SIN(A)
560    MOVE 0,0
570    DRAW 150*COS(A),150*SIN(A)
580    FOR z=1 TO p:NEXT z
590    p=p+1
600 WEND
610 PRINT CHR$(23)+CHR$(0);
620 MOVE 0,0:DRAW 170*COS(A),170*SIN(A)
630 MOVE 0,0:DRAW 170*COS(A+0.01),170*SIN(A+0.01)
640 LOCATE 1,1
650 END
660 PRINT CHR$(7);
670 RETURN
```

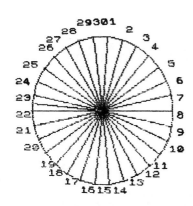

P70 Dog Race

In this program we introduce you to the Amstrad dog track. It can be profitable to play the part of the bookie when running the program.

COMMANDS

Key in the program and RUN.
Follow instructions.

```
100 REM Program - Dog Race
110 CLS
120 SYMBOL 244,4,6,132,252,124,202,169,169
130 SYMBOL 245,224,224,224,224,224,224,224,224
140 SYMBOL 246,255,255,255,224,224,224,224,224
150 DIM d(10),c(10),p(10)
160 REM Select colours for dogs
170 MODE 1
180 FOR i=1 TO 10:c(i)=i+1:NEXT i
190 LOCATE 14,1 : PRINT "RACE NIGHT"
200 LOCATE 10,4 : PRINT "GOOD EVENING FOLKS!"
210 LOCATE 12,6 : PRINT "WELCOME TO THE"
220 LOCATE 11,8 : PRINT "CPC464 DOG TRACK"
230 LOCATE 10,12 : PRINT "Tonight we have a race"
240 LOCATE 10,14 : PRINT "with ten dogs"
250 LOCATE 10,20 : PRINT "Press any key to start"
260 z$=INKEY$:IF z$="" THEN 260
270 MODE 0
280 REM place the traps
290 FOR i=1 TO 10
300   PEN i+1
310   LOCATE 1,2*i+2 : PRINT i-1
320   LOCATE 3,2*i+2 : PRINT CHR$(245)
330 NEXT i
340 LOCATE 1,24 : PRINT "Press key to start";
350 z$=INKEY$:IF z$="" THEN 350
360 LOCATE 1,24 : PRINT "                   ";
370 FOR i=1 TO 10
380   PEN i+1
390   LOCATE 3,2*i+2 : PRINT CHR$(246);
400   d(i)=4
410   PEN c(i) : LOCATE d(i),2*i+2 : PRINT CHR$(244)
420 NEXT i
430 fins=0
440 WHILE fins<10
450   got=1
460   WHILE got=1
470     p=INT(RND(10)*10+1):got=0
480     FOR i=1 TO 10
490       IF p=p(i) THEN got=1
500     NEXT i
```

```
510   WEND
520   LOCATE d(p),2*p+2:PRINT " ";:PEN c(p):PRINT CHR$(244)
530   d(p)=d(p)+1
540   IF d(p)=19 THEN p(fins+1)=p:fins=fins+1:PRINT CHR$(7)
550   IF fins=0 THEN GOSUB 710 ELSE LOCATE 1,1:PRINT ";
560 WEND
570 LOCATE 1,1 : PRINT "Press key for result"
580 z$=INKEY$:IF z$="" THEN 580
590 MODE 1:PEN 1
600 PRINT:PRINT
610 PRINT "THE RESULTS WERE:-":PRINT
620 PRINT "1st - ";p(1)-1
630 PRINT "2nd - ";p(2)-1
640 PRINT "3rd - ";p(3)-1
650 PRINT
660 PRINT "In order the rest were"
670 FOR n=4 TO 10
680   PRINT "Dog ";p(n)-1
690 NEXT n
700 END
710 REM Routine to show who is winning
720 first=0
730 FOR k=1 TO 10
740   IF d(k)>d(first) THEN first=k
750 NEXT k
760 LOCATE 1,1 : PRINT "DOG ";first-1;"is winning"
770 RETURN
```

P71 Shuffle

This program shuffles a deck of cards on the screen.

You could consider this program to be the kernel of any card based game.

COMMANDS

Key in the program and RUN.

```
100 REM Program - Shuffle
110 CLS:INK 1,3:INK 2,0:INK 0,9
120 SYMBOL 244,54,127,127,127,62,28,8,0
130 SYMBOL 245,8,28,28,107,127,107,8,28
140 SYMBOL 246,8,28,62,127,62,28,8,0
150 SYMBOL 247,8,28,62,127,127,127,28,62
160 h$=CHR$(244)
170 c$=CHR$(245)
180 d$=CHR$(246)
190 s$=CHR$(247)
200 pack$=""
210 heart$=""
220 club$=""
230 diamond$=""
240 spade$=""
250 hand1$=""
260 hand2$=""
270 hand3$=""
280 hand4$=""
290 suit$=heart$:x$=h$
300 GOSUB 680:heart$=suit$
310 suit$=club$:x$=c$
320 GOSUB 680:club$=suit$
330 suit$=diamond$:x$=d$
340 GOSUB 680:diamond$=suit$
350 suit$=spade$:x$=s$
360 GOSUB 680:spade$=suit$
370 pack$=heart$+club$+diamond$+spade$
380 :
390 :
400 LOCATE 15,10:PRINT "SHUFFLING";
410 shuffled$=""
420 FOR i=1 TO 50
430   PRINT ".";
440   p=INT(RND(10)*(53-i)+1)*2-1
450   shuffled$=shuffled$+MID$(pack$,p,2)
460   pack$=LEFT$(pack$,p-1)+MID$(pack$,p+2)
470 NEXT i
480 shuffled$=shuffled$+pack$
490 FOR i=1 TO 13
500   hand1$=hand1$+LEFT$(shuffled$,2)
510   shuffled$=MID$(shuffled$,3)
520   hand2$=hand2$+LEFT$(shuffled$,2)
```

```
530    shuffled$=MID$(shuffled$,3)
540    hand3$=hand3$+LEFT$(shuffled$,2)
550    shuffled$=MID$(shuffled$,3)
560    hand4$=hand4$+LEFT$(shuffled$,2)
570    shuffled$=MID$(shuffled$,3)
580 NEXT i
590 DIM x(4)
600 CLS
610 hand$=hand1$:x=14:y=1:GOSUB 760
620 hand$=hand2$:x=5:y=8:GOSUB 760
630 hand$=hand3$:x=14:y=16:GOSUB 760
640 hand$=hand4$:x=28:y=8:GOSUB 760
650 LOCATE 1,23
660 END
670 :
680 REM routine to set up hand
690 FOR i=2 TO 9
700    suit$=suit$+RIGHT$(STR$(i),1)+x$
710 NEXT i
720 suit$="A"+x$+suit$+"T"+x$+"J"+x$+"Q"+x$+"K"+x$
730 RETURN
740 :
750 :
760 REM Routine to print hand
770 x(1)=x:x(2)=x:x(3)=x:x(4)=x
780 FOR i=1 TO 13
790    card$=MID$(hand$,i*2-1,2)
800    IF RIGHT$(card$,1)=h$ OR RIGHT$(card$,1)=d$
       THEN PEN 1 ELSE PEN 2
810    z=ASC(RIGHT$(card$,1))-243
820    LOCATE x(z),y+z:PRINT card$;
830    x(z)=x(z)+2
840 NEXT i
850 RETURN
```

P72 Magic Matrix

This program is based on an interesting idea presented in Martin Gardener's book "Mathematical Puzzles and Diversions", (Bell, 1964).

The program generates a matrix which is not a magic square but which has some interesting properties.

We have found that this is an amusing party trick, even if the matrix is simply drawn out on a piece of paper. The basic idea is rather simple; see if you can work it out.

COMMANDS

Key in the program and RUN.
Follow instructions.


```
100 REM Program - Magic Matrix
110 CLS
120 PRINT "This program produces a square array"
130 PRINT "with the following interesting property."
140 PRINT
150 PRINT "You are asked to pick any number in"
160 PRINT "the square.  You indicate this by row"
170 PRINT "and column number.  The computer will"
180 PRINT "then block out all other numbers in "
190 PRINT "that row and column.  This continues"
200 PRINT "until only one number remains."
210 PRINT:PRINT:PRINT
220 PRINT "Notice that the sum of the numbers"
230 PRINT "remaining is the same as that at the"
240 PRINT "bottom of the screen."
250 PRINT:PRINT:PRINT
260 PRINT "Press any key to continue"
270 z$=INKEY$:IF z$="" THEN 270
280 CLS
290 DIM x(5,2)
300 FOR i=1 TO 5
310    x(i,1)=INT(RND(10)*30+1)
320    x(i,2)=INT(RND(10)*30+1)
330    sum=sum+x(i,1)+x(i,2)
340 NEXT i
350 DIM a(5,5),row(5),column(5)
360 DEF FNpl$(a)=RIGHT$("   "+STR$(a),3)
370 PRINT "         MAGIC MATRIX"
380 PRINT:PRINT:PRINT
390 FOR i=1 TO 5
400    FOR j=1 TO 5
410       a(i,j)=x(i,2)+x(j,1)
420       PRINT FNpl$(a(i,j));
```

```
430    NEXT j
440    PRINT
450 NEXT i
460 :
470 s$=""
480 FOR j=1 TO 5
490    LOCATE 1,20:PRINT "SUM ="sum
500    LOCATE 1,15:INPUT "Row=";r
510    LOCATE 1,16:INPUT "Column=";c
520    IF row(r)>0 OR column(c)>0 THEN 500
530    row(r)=1:column(c)=1
540    FOR i=1 TO 5
550       LOCATE I*3-2,4+r:PRINT " . "
560       LOCATE 3*c-2,4+i:PRINT " . "
570    NEXT i
580    LOCATE 20,4+r:PRINT a(r,c)
590    s$=s$+"+"+STR$(a(r,c))
600 NEXT j
610 LOCATE 4,21:PRINT "="MID$(s$,2)
620 END
```

```
               MAGIC MATRIX

          .   30   19    .   8
          .    .    .    .   .              18
          .   29   18    .   7
          .    .    .    .   .              16
          .   31   20    .   9


      Sum  =    91
      Row  =  ?  2
      Column   ?  4
```

P73 Encoder

This program can be used to code a secret message. The system used for the encoding is very simple. You are asked for a key word, the characters of which are used to offset the characters of the secret message. The program uses all the normal printable characters of the Amstrad, so that characters such as space, full stop and comma etc are also encoded.

COMMANDS

Key in the program and RUN.
Follow instructions.

```
100 REM PROGRAM - ENCODER
110 DIM offset(25),characters(255),code(255)
120 CLS
130 PRINT :PRINT:PRINT
140 PRINT "This program can be used to produce a"
150 PRINT "coded version of a secret message."
160 PRINT "The program bases the encoding on a key"
170 PRINT "word which you specify."
180 PRINT
190 PRINT : PRINT : PRINT
200 :
210 t=0
220 WHILE t=0
230    PRINT "Please enter your message"
240    PEN 0
250    LINE INPUT message$
260    PEN 2
270    PRINT "Do you wish to see your message?"
280    GOSUB 760
290    IF t=1 THEN PRINT message$
300    PRINT "Is the message OK?"
310    GOSUB 760
320 WEND
330 :
340 CLS
350 t=0
360 WHILE t=0
370    PRINT "Please enter your code word"
380    PEN 0
390    LINE INPUT code$
400    PEN 2
410    PRINT "Do you wish to see your code word?"
420    GOSUB 760
430    IF t=1 THEN PRINT code$
440    PRINT "Is the code word OK?"
450    GOSUB 760
```

```
460 WEND
470 :
480 CLS
490 :
500 FOR i=1 TO LEN(code$)
510    offset(i)=ASC(MID$(code$,i,1))-32
520 NEXT i
530 :
540 FOR i=1 TO LEN(message$)
550    characters(i)=ASC(MID$(message$,i,1))-32
560 NEXT i
570 :
580 REM Encoding routine
590 word$=""
600 j=0
610 FOR i=1 TO LEN(message$)
620    code(i)=(characters(i)+offset(j+1)) MOD 93
630    word$=word$+CHR$(code(i)+32)
640    j=(j+1) MOD LEN(code$)
650 NEXT i
660 :
670 PRINT "Your coded message is "
680 PRINT word$
690 PRINT : PRINT : PRINT
700 PRINT "Press any key to clear"
710 a$=INKEY$:IF a$="" THEN 710
720 CLS
730 END
740 :
750 :
760 REM Subroutine to test Y/N
770 REM routine returns t=1 if Y
780 REM                  t=0 if N
790 fin=0
800 WHILE fin=0
810    a$=INKEY$:IF a$="" THEN 810
820    IF a$="Y" OR a$="y" THEN t=1:fin=1
830    IF a$="N" OR a$="n" THEN t=0:fin=1
840 WEND
850 RETURN
```

P74 Decoder

This program can be used to decode the secret message found using the encoder program. You need to have the secret message plus the key word to find the original message.

COMMANDS

Key in program and RUN.
Follow instructions


```
100 REM PROGRAM - DECODER
110 DIM offset(25),characters(255),code(255)
120 CLS
130 PRINT :PRINT:PRINT
140 PRINT "This program can be used to produce a"
150 PRINT "decoded version of a secret message."
160 PRINT "The program bases the decoding on a key"
170 PRINT "word which you specify."
180 PRINT
190 PRINT : PRINT : PRINT
200 :
210 t=0
220 WHILE t=0
230    PRINT "Please enter your coded message"
240    PEN 0
250    LINE INPUT message$
260    PEN 2
270    PRINT "Do you wish to see your message?"
280    GOSUB 770
290    IF t=1 THEN PRINT message$
300    PRINT "Is the message OK?"
310    GOSUB 770
320 WEND
330 :
340 CLS
350 t=0
360 WHILE t=0
370    PRINT "Please enter your code word"
380    PEN 0
390    LINE INPUT code$
400    PEN 2
410    PRINT "Do you wish to see your code word?"
420    GOSUB 770
430    IF t=1 THEN PRINT code$
440    PRINT "Is the code word OK?"
450    GOSUB 770
460 WEND
470 :
480 CLS
490 :
```

```
500 FOR i=1 TO LEN(code$)
510    offset(i)=ASC(MID$(code$,i,1))-32
520 NEXT i
530 :
540 FOR i=1 TO LEN(message$)
550    characters(i)=ASC(MID$(message$,i,1))-32
560 NEXT i
570 :
580 REM Decoding routine
590 word$=""
600 j=0
610 FOR i=1 TO LEN(message$)
620    code(i)=(characters(i)-offset(j+1)) MOD 93
630    IF code(i)<0 THEN code(i)=93+code(i)
640    word$=word$+CHR$(code(i)+32)
650    j=(j+1) MOD LEN(code$)
660 NEXT i
670 :
680 PRINT "Your coded message is "
690 PRINT word$
700 PRINT : PRINT : PRINT
710 PRINT "Press any key to clear"
720 a$=INKEY$:IF a$="" THEN 720
730 CLS
740 END
750 :
760 :
770 REM Subroutine to test Y/N
780 REM routine returns t=1 if Y
790 REM               t=0 if N
800 fin=0
810 WHILE fin=0
820    a$=INKEY$:IF a$="" THEN 820
830    IF a$="Y" OR a$="y" THEN t=1:fin=1
840    IF a$="N" OR a$="n" THEN t=0:fin=1
850 WEND
860 RETURN
```

P75 Number of Days

It can be interesting in many everyday problems to calculate
the number of days between two dates. This program does this
by calculating the number of days from day zero of the
Gregorian Calendar for each date and then calculating the
number of days between the two dates.

COMMANDS

Key in the program and type RUN.
Enter Gregorian dates when prompted.


```
100 REM Program - Number of Days
110 DEFINT d,m,y
120 CLS
130 PRINT : PRINT : PRINT
140 PRINT "This program calculates the number "
150 PRINT "of days between two dates."
160 PRINT:PRINT:PRINT
170 PRINT "The program uses the Gregorian calendar"
180 PRINT : PRINT : PRINT
190 PRINT "Enter first date of interest"
200 d1=0:m1=0:y1=0
210 WHILE d1<1 OR d1>31
220    INPUT "Day (1-31)"; d1
230 WEND
240 WHILE m1<1 OR m1>12
250    INPUT "Month (1-12)";m1
260 WEND
270 WHILE y1<1
280    INPUT "Year (eg 1985)";y1
290 WEND
300 dd=d1:mm=m1:yy=y1:GOSUB 520
310 n1=nn
320 :
330 PRINT : PRINT "Enter second date of interest"
340 d2=0:m2=0:y2=0
350 WHILE d2<1 OR d2>31
360    INPUT "Day (1-31)"; d2
370 WEND
380 WHILE m2<1 OR m2>12
390    INPUT "Month (1-12)";m2
400 WEND
410 WHILE y2<1
420    INPUT "Year (eg 1985)";y2
430 WEND
440 dd=d2:mm=m2:yy=y2:GOSUB 520
450 n2=nn
460 IF n1>n2 THEN no=n1-n2 ELSE no=n2-n1
470 PRINT "Number of days between the two dates is"
480 PRINT no
```

```
490 END
500 :
510 :
520 REM Subroutine to calculate no of
530 REM days since day zero
540 REM
550 REM INPUTS : dd,mm,yy
560 REM OUTPUT - nn
570 RESTORE
580 FOR i=1 TO mm
590   READ dty
600 NEXT i
610 DATA 0,31,59,90,120,151,181,212,243,273,304,334
620 dty=dty + dd
630 nn=dty + yy*365 + INT(yy/4) +1 - INT(yy/100) + INT(yy/400)
640 IF (yy MOD 4 =0) AND mm<3 THEN nn=nn-1
650 RETURN
```

P76 Pools Programme

This program selects random numbers to help you fill up four treble chance columns on a football pools coupon.

We've not won yet!!!!

COMMANDS

Key in the program and RUN.
Follow instructions.

```
100 REM Program - Pools Program
110 DIM temp%(100)
120 DEF FNpl$(a)=RIGHT$("   "+STR$(a),3)
130 CLS
140 PRINT : PRINT : PRINT
150 PRINT "This program will not win the pools"
160 PRINT "for you.  It does not reduce the odds in"
170 PRINT "any way, but it does remove the"
180 PRINT "responsibility of losing from you."
190 PRINT "The program will present you with your"
200 PRINT "treble chance numbers."
210 :
220 PRINT:PRINT:PRINT
230 INPUT "How many games on entry form";games
240 INPUT "How many columns are you entering";columns
250 INPUT "How many entries in each column";entries
260 :
270 CLS
280 FOR i=1 TO columns
290    j=1
300    WHILE j<entries+1
310       temp%(j)=INT(RND(10)*games+1)
320       flag=0
330       FOR k=1 TO j-1
340         IF temp%(k)=temp%(j) THEN flag=1
350       NEXT k
360       IF flag=0 THEN LOCATE i*5,j:PRINT FNpl$(temp%(j)):j=j+1
370    WEND
380 NEXT i
390 END
```

4	33	30
2	5	1
23	36	24
27	19	28
7	3	12
35	32	32
10	26	33
19	21	31
8	18	25
16	25	36
11	22	14
1	11	8

P77 Kitchen Timer

A useful program for the kitchen here - it lets you know how long it will be before a meal is ready. At the end of the period specified an alarm sounds.

COMMANDS

Key in the program and RUN.
Enter the delay required when prompted.

```
100 REM Program - Kitchen Timer
110 CLS
120 PRINT:PRINT:PRINT
130 PRINT "What setting do you require ?"
140 INPUT "Hours ";hours
150 INPUT "Minutes ";mins
160 INPUT "Seconds ";secs
170 IF secs>0 THEN secs=secs-1
180 MODE 0
190 :
200 EVERY 50 GOSUB 480
210 t=TIME
220 WHILE hours<>-1
230    WHILE mins<>-1
240      WHILE secs<>-1
250        t=TIME
260        WHILE TIME-t<300
270        WEND
280        LOCATE 5,12:PRINT hours
290        LOCATE 8,12:PRINT mins
300        LOCATE 11,12:PRINT secs
310        secs=secs-1
320      WEND
330      mins=mins-1
340      secs=59
350    WEND
360    hours=hours-1
370    mins=59
380 WEND
390 :
400 FOR i=1 TO 10
410    PRINT CHR$(7)
420    FOR j=1 TO 10
430    NEXT j
440 NEXT i
450 CLS
460 LOCATE 8,12:PRINT "FINISHED"
470 END
480 LOCATE 8,12:PRINT ":"
490 LOCATE 11,12:PRINT ":"
500 RETURN
```

P78 School Report

This program prepares a school report for a student. The program could be developed to store data on a tape or disk file and handle more than one student.

COMMANDS

Key in the program and RUN.
Enter details as requested.


```
100 REM Program - School Report
110 MODE 2  'using 80 column as printer
120 BORDER 6
130 PRINT : PRINT : PRINT
140 PRINT SPACE$(34);"SCHOOL REPORT"
150 PRINT:PRINT:PRINT
160 PRINT SPACE$(23);"PLEASE ENSURE THAT YOUR PRINTER"
170 PRINT:PRINT SPACE$(23);"HAS BEEN SET UP CORRECTLY"
180 LOCATE 10,20:PRINT "PRESS KEY WHEN READY"
190 z$=INKEY$:IF z$="" THEN 190
200 GOSUB 710                       'draw out background
210 w$="":wdth=20:px=12:py=3:GOSUB 870
220 student$=w$
230 w$="":wdth=20:px=47:py=3:GOSUB 870
240 school$=w$
250 w$="":wdth=20:px=48:py=5:GOSUB 870
260 session$=w$
270 DIM subject$(10),attendp$(10),attenta$(10),
        grade$(10),posn$(10),comment$(10)
280 sub=8:attp=4:atta=4:grade=2:posn=3:comment=30
290 FOR i=1 TO 10
300    px=4:py=9+i:wdth=sub
310    GOSUB 870
320    subject$(i)=w$+SPACE$(8-LEN(w$))
330    IF LEN(w$)=0 THEN PRINT CHR$(7):i=10:GOTO 440
340    px=14:py=9+i:wdth=attp:GOSUB 870
350    attendp$(i)=w$+SPACE$(4-LEN(w$))
360    px=19:py=9+i:wdth=atta:GOSUB 870
370    attenda$(i)=w$+SPACE$(4-LEN(w$))
380    px=27:py=9+i:wdth=grade:GOSUB 870
390    grade$(i)=w$+SPACE$(2-LEN(w$))
400    px=36:py=9+i:wdth=posn:GOSUB 870
410    posn$(i)=w$+SPACE$(3-LEN(w$))
420    px=43:py=9+i:wdth=comment:GOSUB 870
430    comment$(i)=w$+SPACE$(30-LEN(w$))
440 NEXT i
450 px=23:py=22:wdth=20:GOSUB 870
460 overall$=w$
470 px=20:py=24:wdth=2:GOSUB 870
480 ans$=w$
490 IF UPPER$(ans$)="N" THEN RUN
500 :
```

```
510 REM now print out the report
520 CLS
530 LOCATE 10,10:PRINT "Please align paper, then press any key"
540 z$=INKEY$:IF z$="" THEN 540
550 PRINT#8, SPC(40);"SCHOOL REPORT"
560 PRINT#8, :PRINT #8, :PRINT#8,""
570 PRINT#8, "STUDENT - ";student$;SPC(10);" SESSION - ";SESSION$
580 PRINT #8, :PRINT #8, :PRINT#8,
590 PRINT#8, "SUBJECT    ATTENDANCE  GRADE  POSITION    COMMENT"
600 PRINT#8,"            P    A              IN CLASS"
610 PRINT#8, : PRINT #8,: PRINT#8,""
620 FOR I=1 TO 10
630    PRINT#8, subject$(i);SPC(4);attendp$(i);" ";attenda$(i);
              SPC(4);grade$(i);SPC(6);posn$(i);SPC(6);comment$(i)
640 NEXT i
650 PRINT#8, : PRINT#8, : PRINT#8,""
660 PRINT#8, "OVERALL ASSESSMENT - ";overall$
670 PRINT#8,:PRINT #8,
680 PRINT #8,"SIGNATURE OF PARENT OR GUARDIAN - ";STRING$(20,"_")
690 END
700 REM Background of report
710 CLS
720 LOCATE 34,1:PRINT "SCHOOL REPORT"
730 LOCATE 3,3:PRINT
    "STUDENT :            :          SCHOOL :                :"
740 LOCATE 39,5:PRINT "SESSION :              :"
750 LOCATE 3,7:
    PRINT "SUBJECT     ATTENDANCE  GRADE  POSITION     COMMENT"
760 LOCATE 3,8:PRINT "            P    A              IN CLASS"
770 LOCATE 3,22:PRINT "OVERALL ASSESSMENT :             :"
780 LOCATE 3,24:PRINT "REPORT OK (Y/N) : :"
790 MOVE 16,400-6*16+4:DRAW 608,400-6*16+4
800 MOVE 16,400-20*16+4:DRAW 608,400-20*16+4
810 MOVE 16,400-8*16-4:DRAW 608,400-8*16-4
820 MOVE 16,400-6*16+4:DRAWR 0,-14*16:MOVER 9*8,0:DRAWR 0,14*16
830 MOVER 13*8,0:DRAWR 0,-14*16:MOVER 7*8,0:DRAWR 0,14*16
840 MOVER 10*8,0:DRAWR 0,-14*16:MOVER 35*8,0:DRAWR 0,14*16
850 RETURN
860 REM Routine to get field
870 c=1:z$="":LOCATE px,py:w$=""
880 WHILE c<wdth AND z$<>CHR$(13)
890    PRINT CHR$(233);
900    z$=INKEY$:IF z$="" THEN 900
910    PRINT CHR$(8);
920    IF z$=CHR$(127) THEN PRINT CHR$(8)+" "+CHR$(8);:
                     w$=LEFT$(w$,c-2):c=c-1:GOTO 950
930    IF z$<> CHR$(13) THEN w$=w$+z$:PRINT z$;
940    c=c+1
950 WEND
960 PRINT " ";
970 RETURN
```

SCHOOL REPORT

STUDENT - John Gordon   SESSION - 1986-1987

SUBJECT	ATTENDANCE P A	GRADE	POSITION IN CLASS	COMMENT
Maths	50 45	a	3	Very Good
English	50 48	f	14	Not so good

OVERALL ASSESSMENT - Could be better

SIGNATURE OF PARENT OR GUARDIAN - _____

P79 Counting

This program could be useful for the very young schoolchild. It displays up to nine monsters on the screen. The user is required to count the monsters and press the appropriate numeric key. The RETURN key is not used.

The program could be expanded so that several groups of items (say monsters, flowers and automobiles) appear on the screen at the same time and the user is asked to count the numbers in one particular group.

COMMANDS

Key in the program and RUN.
Stop the program by pressing the space bar as instructed.

```
100 REM Program - Counting
110 ENV 1,5,3,4,2,-4,4,3,2,4,1,0,12,2,-3,4
120 DIM x(10),y(10)
130 DEF FNrand(d)=FIX(RND(TIME)*d)+1
140 MODE 0:PAPER 2:CLS:BORDER 6
150 SYMBOL 244,24,60,90,126,36,90,66,129
160 PEN 1
170 :
180 WHILE 1=1
190   count=FIX(RND(TIME)*9)+1
200   INK 2,2:CLS
210   x(1)=FNrand(20)
220   y(1)=FNrand(22)
230   :
240   FOR i=2 TO count
250     x(i)=FNrand(20)
260     y(i)=FNrand(22)
270     FOR j=1 TO i-1
280       IF x(i)=x(j) AND y(i)=y(j) THEN i=i-1
290     NEXT j
300   NEXT i
310   :
320   FOR i=1 TO count
330     LOCATE x(i),y(i):PRINT CHR$(244);
340   NEXT i
350   :
360   flag=0
370   WHILE flag=0
380     flag=-1
390     LOCATE 1,24:PRINT "How many monsters";
400     ans$=INKEY$:IF ans$="" THEN 400
410     LOCATE 1,24:PRINT SPACE$(30);
420     ans=VAL(ans$)
430     IF ans=count THEN INK 2,5,8:GOSUB 470
          ELSE  SOUND 1,200,10,0,1,0,4:flag=0
```

```
440     WEND
450 WEND
460 END
470 tempo=2.5
480    RESTORE 570
490    FOR x=1 TO 20
500      READ pitch,duration
510      pitch=pitch-140
520      freq=440*(2^((pitch-10)/12))
530      pitchnum=ROUND(125000/freq)
540      SOUND 1,pitchnum,duration*tempo,15,0,0,0
550    NEXT x
560 RETURN
570 DATA 109,6,117,2,121,6,129,2,137,8,157,6,165,2,
           169,8,165,6,157,8,137,8
580 DATA 109,6,117,2,121,6,129,2,137,8,157,4,110,2,
           137,2,145,8
```

How many monsters

P80 Arithmetic Tutorial

This is the bare bones of a tutorial program which could be used in a primary school class. The program allows the pupil to have practice in simple arithmetic problems. Routines have been implemented to handle multiplication, division, addition and subtraction.

COMMANDS

Key in the program and RUN.


```
100 REM Program - Arithmetic Tutor
110 MODE 1
120 SYMBOL 244,4,4,4,4,4,4,4,4,4
130 SYMBOL 245,4,7,0,0,0,0,0,0,0
140 SYMBOL 246,0,255,0,0,0,0,0,0,0
150 :
160 res$="Y"
170 WHILE UPPER$(res$)="Y"
180    CLS
190    PRINT "You will be presented with an"
200    PRINT "arithmetic problem. Solve the problem"
210    PRINT "by keying in your solution in the"
220    PRINT "normal manner."
230    PRINT:PRINT
240    PRINT "Problems can be given in:":PRINT
250    PRINT "1. Addition"
260    PRINT "2. Subtraction"
270    PRINT "3. Division"
280    PRINT "4. Multiplication"
290    PRINT:PRINT
300    INPUT "Make your choice ";choice
310    ON choice GOSUB 610,700,790,1100
320    PRINT:PRINT:PRINT
330    INPUT "Another run ";res$
340 WEND
350 END
360 n1$=STR$(num1)
370 n2$=STR$(num2)
380 WHILE INKEY$<>"":WEND
390 LOCATE 1,12:PRINT SPC(20-LEN(n1$));n1$
400 LOCATE 1,15:PRINT SPC(18-LEN(n2$));s$;n2$;
410 LOCATE 16,16:PRINT STRING$(5,"_");
420 correct=0
430 WHILE NOT correct
440    b$=""
450    p=20
460    a$=" "
470    WHILE ASC(a$)<>13
480       correct=0
490       a$=INKEY$:IF a$="" THEN 490
```

```
500      IF ASC(a$)<>13 THEN b$=a$+b$:LOCATE p,19:PRINT a$;:p=p-1
510   WEND
520   IF VAL(b$)=result
         THEN LOCATE 5,22:PRINT "CORRECT - WELL DONE":correct=-1
         ELSE LOCATE 5,22:PRINT "WRONG - TRY AGAIN"
530   t=TIME
540   WHILE TIME-t<900:WEND
550   LOCATE 5,19:PRINT SPACE$(20);
560   LOCATE 5,20:PRINT SPACE$(20);
570 WEND
580 RETURN
590 :
600 :
610 REM Addition
620 num1=FIX(RND(TIME)*999)+1
630 num2=FIX(RND(TIME)*999)+1
640 CLS
650 PRINT:PRINT:PRINT "      ADDITION"
660 s$="+ ":result=num1+num2:GOSUB 360
670 RETURN
680 :
690 :
700 REM Subtraction
710 num1=FIX(RND(TIME)*999)+1
720 num2=FIX(RND(TIME)*num1)+1
730 CLS
740 PRINT:PRINT:PRINT "      SUBTRACTION"
750 s$="- ":result=num1-num2:GOSUB 360
760 RETURN
770 :
780 :
790 REM Division
800 CLS
810 num2=3:num1=1
820 WHILE FIX(num1/num2)<>num1/num2
830    num2=FIX(RND(TIME)*9)+1
835    num1=(FIX(RND(TIME)*99)+1)*num2
840    IF num2=0 THEN 830
860 WEND
870 PRINT:PRINT:PRINT "      DIVISION"
880 n1$=STR$(num1)
890 n2$=STR$(num2)
900 LOCATE 10,12:PRINT n2$;CHR$(244);n1$;
910 LOCATE 12,13:PRINT CHR$(245);STRING$(5,CHR$(246))
920 correct=0
930 WHILE NOT correct
940    b$=""
950    p=14:a$=" "
960    WHILE ASC(a$)<>13
970      correct=0
980      a$=INKEY$:IF a$="" THEN 980
990      IF ASC(a$)<>13
            THEN b$=b$+a$:LOCATE p,14:PRINT a$;:p=p+1
1000     WEND
1010     IF VAL(b$)=num1/num2
            THEN LOCATE 5,22:PRINT "CORRECT - WELL DONE":correct=
            ELSE LOCATE 5,22:PRINT "WRONG - TRY AGAIN"
```

```
1020     t=TIME
1030     WHILE TIME-t<900:WEND
1040     LOCATE 5,14:PRINT STRING$(20," ");
1050     LOCATE 5,22:PRINT STRING$(20," ");
1060 WEND
1070 RETURN
1080 :
1090 :
1100 REM Multiplication
1110 CLS
1120 num1=FIX(RND(TIME)*999)+1
1130 num2=FIX(RND(TIME)*9)+1
1140 PRINT:PRINT:PRINT "          MULTIPLICATION"
1150 s$="* ":result=num1*num2:GOSUB 360
1160 RETURN
```

P81 French Tutorial

This program gives the French implementation of a language vocabulary tutorial. In both cases the data are in the form of word pairs which may be inserted by the teacher as data statements.

The program gives the student up to three attempts at each word. After the tutorial is finished statistics are returned.

The program could be extended so that several alternative answers may be accepted for some words.

COMMANDS

Key in the program and RUN.
Follow the instructions.


```
100 REM Program - French Tutorial
110 DIM results(4)
120 MODE 1:BORDER 7:INK 2,21:PAPER 2:CLS
130 LOCATE 10,10:PRINT "FRENCH TUTORIAL"
140 t=TIME
150 WHILE TIME-t<900:WEND
160 RESTORE
170 :
180 english$=" "
190 WHILE english$<>"end"
200    attempt=1
210    READ english$,french$
220    answer$=" "
230    WHILE answer$<>french$ AND attempt<5
240       CLS
250       LOCATE 1,6
260       PRINT "Attempt number ";attempt
270       PRINT:PRINT
280       PRINT "English word is ";english$
290       PRINT:PRINT
300       INPUT "What is the French ";answer$
310       attempt=attempt+1
320    WEND
330    IF answer$<>french$ THEN results(4)=results(4)+1
       ELSE results(attempt-1)=results(attempt-1)+1
340 WEND
350 :
360 CLS
370 PRINT:PRINT:PRINT
380 PRINT "Number correct at first attempt is ";results(1)
390 PRINT "Number correct at second attempt is ";results(2)
400 PRINT "Number correct at third attempt is ";results(3)
410 PRINT "Number of unknown answers ";results(4)
```

```
420 END
430 :
440 DATA yes,oui,no,non,end,fin
```

P82 Italian Tutorial

This program gives the Italian implementation of a language vocabulary tutorial. The data are in the form of word pairs which may be inserted by the teacher as data statements.

This program is a little bit more sophisticated than the French tutorial in that a list is maintained of questions still to be answered correctly at the first attempt. If the student gets a question wrong, it is re-inserted later in the list. At the end of the session a report is given.

The program could be extended so that several alternative answers may be accepted for some words.

COMMANDS

Key in the program and RUN.
Follow the instructions.

```
100 REM Program - Italian Tutorial
110 DIM results(4)
120 MODE 1:BORDER 7:INK 2,21:PAPER 2:CLS
130 LOCATE 10,10:PRINT "ITALIAN TUTORIAL"
140 t=TIME
150 :
160 WHILE TIME-t<900:WEND
170 :
180 READ no.of.words:count=no.of.words
190 DIM eng$(no.of.words),ital$(no.of.words),
        plist(no.of.words)
200 :
210 FOR j=1 TO no.of.words
220    READ eng$(j),ital$(j)
230    plist(j)=j
240 NEXT j
250 :
260 j=1
270 WHILE count>0
280    attempt=0
290    answer$=" "
300    WHILE answer$<>ital$(plist(j)) AND attempt<4
310       CLS
320       LOCATE 1,6
330       PRINT "Attempt number ";attempt+1
340       PRINT:PRINT
350       PRINT "English word is ";eng$(plist(j))
360       PRINT:PRINT
370       INPUT "What is the Italian ";answer$
380       attempt=attempt+1
390    WEND
```

```
400   IF answer$<>ital$(plist(j)) THEN results(4)=results(4)+1:
      PRINT "WRONG- correct answer is "ital$(plist(j)):
      GOSUB 610:GOTO 450
410   IF attempt=1 THEN PRINT "Correct ":count=count-1:j=j+1
420   IF attempt=2 THEN PRINT "Correct ":GOSUB 700
      'end of list routine
430   IF attempt=3 THEN PRINT "Correct ":GOSUB 610
      'middle of list routine
440   results(attempt)=results(attempt)+1
450   LOCATE 1,15
460   PRINT "Press key to continue"
470   z$=INKEY$:IF z$="" THEN 470
480 WEND
490 :
500 CLS
510 PRINT:PRINT:PRINT
520 PRINT "Number correct at first attempt is ";results(1)
530 PRINT "Number correct at second attempt is ";results(2)
540 PRINT "Number correct at third attempt is ";results(3)
550 PRINT:PRINT:PRINT "The number of words were ";no.of.words
560 PRINT:PRINT "You effectively used ";
                 results(1)+results(2)+results(3)+results(4);
                 " words"
570 PRINT:PRINT "Your score is then ";
    no.of.words*10-(results(2)*2+results(3)*4+results(4)*8)
580 END
590 :
600 REM Middle of list routine
610 no.left=no.of.words-j-1
620 posn=j+FIX(RND(TIME)*no.left)+1
630 temp=plist(j)
640 FOR k=j TO posn-1
650    plist(k)=plist(k+1)
660 NEXT k
670 plist(posn)=temp
680 RETURN
690 REM End of list routine
700 posn=no.of.words
710 temp=plist(j)
720 FOR k=j TO posn-1
730    plist(k)=plist(k+1)
740 NEXT k
750 plist(posn)=temp
760 RETURN
770 DATA 4,apparatus,apparecchio,barley,orzo
780 DATA chair,sedia,dialect,dialetto
790 DATA ear,orecchio,flour,farina
800 DATA glove,guanto,hymn,inno
810 DATA important,importante,jungle,giungla
```

P83 Number Base Conversion

This is a very useful program for work in a computing laboratory. It allows you to convert numbers from one base to another.

COMMANDS

Key in the program and RUN.
Select the conversion you require.


```
10 REM Number base conversion
20 PAPER 0:INK 0,1
30 PEN 1:INK 1,24
40 BORDER 1
50 MODE 1
60 PRINT TAB(9)"NUMBER BASE CONVERSION"
70 PRINT TAB(9)"************************"
80 PRINT:PRINT:PRINT
90 PRINT"This program deals with integer numbers"
100 PRINT"in the range 0 to 65535."
110 GOSUB 1200:REM Any key
120 :
130 WHILE a%<>5
140 :   a%=0
150 :   CLS
160 :   PRINT"To select  the  conversion  you require"
170 :   PRINT"press one of the following keys:"
180 :   LOCATE 1,8
190 :   PRINT TAB(4)"Key 1 - Hex to decimal"
200 :   PRINT
210 :   PRINT TAB(4)"Key 2 - Decimal to hex"
220 :   PRINT
230 :   PRINT TAB(4)"Key 3 - Binary to decimal"
240 :   PRINT
250 :   PRINT TAB(4)"Key 4 - Decimal to binary"
260 :   PRINT
270 :   PRINT TAB(4)"Key 5 - Ends program."
280 :
290 :   WHILE a%>5 OR a%<1
300 :     a$=INKEY$:IF a$="" THEN 300
310 :     a%=ASC(a$)-48
320 :   WEND
330 :
340 :   bad=1
350 :   ON a% GOSUB 420,670,800,1010
360 WEND
370 CLS
380 END
390 :
400 :
410 REM Hex to decimal
```

```
420 WHILE bad=1
430 :   CLS
440 :   PRINT TAB(13)"HEX TO DECIMAL"
450 :   PRINT:PRINT:PRINT
460 :   INPUT "What is the hex number";h$
470 :   dc=0
480 :   h$=UPPER$(h$)
490 :   FOR n=1 TO LEN(h$)
500 :     hx=ASC(MID$(h$,n,1))
510 :     bad=1
520 :     IF hx>47 AND hx<58 THEN hx=hx-48:bad=0
530 :     IF hx>64 AND hx<71 THEN hx=hx-55:bad=0
540 :     IF bad=1 THEN n=LEN(h$)
550 :     d=hx*16^(LEN(h$)-n)
560 :     dc=dc+d
570 :   NEXT
580 :   IF LEN(h$)>4 THEN bad=1
590 WEND
600 PRINT:PRINT
610 PRINT"Decimal number is";dc
620 GOSUB 1200
630 RETURN
640 :
650 :
660 REM Decimal to hex
670 WHILE bad=1
680 :   CLS
690 :   PRINT TAB(13)"DECIMAL TO HEX"
700 :   GOSUB 1130:REM Decimal range check
710 WEND
720 PRINT:PRINT
730 PRINT"Hexadecimal number is ";HEX$(decn)
740 GOSUB 1200
750 RETURN
760 :
770 :
780 :
790 REM Binary to decimal
800 WHILE bad=1
810 :   CLS
820 :   PRINT TAB(11)"BINARY TO DECIMAL"
830 :   PRINT:PRINT:PRINT
840 :   INPUT "Binary number";b$
850 :   dc=0
860 :   FOR n=1 TO LEN(b$)
870 :     bn=ASC(MID$(b$,n,1))
880 :     IF bn>47 AND bn<50 THEN bn=bn-48:bad=0:ELSE bad=1
890 :     IF bad=1 THEN n=LEN(b$)
900 :     d=bn*2^(LEN(b$)-n)
910 :     dc=dc+d
920 :   NEXT
930 :   IF LEN(b$)>16 THEN bad=1
940 WEND
950 PRINT:PRINT
960 PRINT"Decimal number is";dc
970 GOSUB 1200
980 RETURN
```

```
990 :
1000 REM Decimal to binary
1010 WHILE bad=1
1020 :   CLS
1030 :   PRINT TAB(11)"DECIMAL TO BINARY"
1040 :   GOSUB 1130:REM Decimal range check
1050 WEND
1060 PRINT:PRINT
1070 PRINT"Binary number is ";BIN$(decn,16)
1080 GOSUB 1200
1090 RETURN
1100 :
1110 :
1120 REM Decimal range check
1130 PRINT:PRINT:PRINT
1140 INPUT "What is the decimal number";decn
1150 IF decn>-1 AND decn<65536 THEN bad=0
1160 RETURN
1170 :
1180 :
1190 REM Any key
1200 PRINT:PRINT:PRINT
1210 PRINT"Press any key for menu."
1220 a$=INKEY$:IF a$="" THEN 1220
1230 RETURN
```

P84 Colour Codes For Resistors

This program could be useful in an electronics laboratory.
It allows you to calculate the value of a resistor from its
colour code, or to calculate the colour code from its value.
The program deals only with resistors coded by colour bands
as shown below:

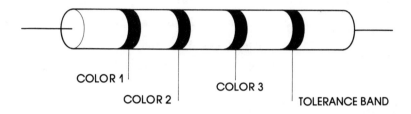

COLOR 1
COLOR 2
COLOR 3
TOLERANCE BAND

COMMANDS

Key in the program and RUN.
Follow the instructions.

```
10 REM Colour codes for resistors
20 PEN 1:INK 1,24
30 PAPER 0:INK 0,1
40 BORDER 1
50 MODE 1
60 PRINT TAB(10)"RESISTOR COLOUR CODES"
70 PRINT TAB(10)"*********************"
80 LOCATE 1,6
90 PRINT"This program may be used to determine"
100 PRINT"the value of a resistor from its colour"
110 PRINT"code, or to determine its colour code"
120 PRINT"from its resistance value."
130 :
140 DIM b$(13):REM Holds colours
150 FOR n=1 TO 13
160 :   READ b$(n)
170 NEXT
180 :
190 DATA black,brown,red,orange,yellow,green
200 DATA blue,violet,grey,white,gold,silver,none
210 :
220 GOSUB 1470:REM Any key
230 :
240 :
```

```
250 WHILE a<>3
260 :   CLS
270 :   LOCATE 1,4
280 :   PRINT"Do you wish to find resistance value or"
290 :   PRINT"colour code?"
300 :   LOCATE 8,8
310 :   PRINT"Press key 1 for value
320 :   PRINT
330 :   PRINT TAB(8);"Press key 2 for code"
340 :   PRINT
350 :   PRINT TAB(8);"Press key 3 to end"
360 :   a$="4"
370 :   WHILE a$<>"1" AND a$<>"2" AND a$<>"3"
380 :     a$=INKEY$
390 :   WEND
400 :   a=VAL(a$)
410 :   ON a GOSUB 480,1020
420 WEND
430 CLS
440 END
450 :
460 :
470 REM Value
480 flag=1
490 WHILE flag=1
500 :   CLS
510 :   PRINT TAB(14);"COLOURS ARE"
520 :   PRINT
530 :   FOR n=0 TO 9
540 :     PRINT,b$(n+1),"=";n
550 :   NEXT
560 :   PRINT:PRINT
570 :   PRINT"Enter the three colour bands as three"
580 :   PRINT"numbers followed by the ENTER key."
590 :   PRINT:PRINT
600 :   PRINT"For example:"
610 :   PRINT"red-black-orange = 203"
620 :   PRINT
630 :   INPUT"What are the colours";cl$
640 :
650 :   FOR n=1 TO LEN(cl$)
660 :     d(n)=ASC(MID$(cl$,n,1))-48
670 :     IF d(n)<0 OR d(n)>9 THEN flag=1 ELSE flag=0
680 :     IF flag=1 THEN n=LEN(cl$)
690 :   NEXT
700 :   IF LEN(cl$)<>3 THEN flag=1
710 WEND
720 :
730 CLS
740 LOCATE 1,3
750 PRINT"The third band indicates tolerance. The"
760 PRINT"alternatives are:"
770 PRINT:PRINT
780 FOR n=11 TO 13
790 :   PRINT,n-10,b$(n)
800 NEXT
810 PRINT:PRINT
```

```
820 PRINT"Enter 1,2 or 3 to select tolerance"
830 PRINT"colour. Any other entry will be treated"
840 PRINT"as no fourth band.
850 PRINT:PRINT
860 INPUT"Selection (1, 2 or 3)";t$
870 IF t$<>"1" AND t$<>"2" THEN t$="3"
880 t=5*VAL(t$)
890 IF t=15 THEN t=20
900 :
910 res=(10*d(1)+d(2))*10^d(3)
920 CLS
930 LOCATE 4,4
940 PRINT"Resistance is";res;"ohm"
950 LOCATE 4,7
960 PRINT"Tolerance is";t;"%"
970 GOSUB 1470:REM Any key
980 RETURN
990 :
1000 :
1010 REM Get code
1020 flag=1
1030 WHILE flag=1
1040 :   CLS
1050 :   LOCATE 1,4
1060 :   PRINT"Please enter the resistance in ohm."
1070 :   PRINT"Please enter numbers only."
1080 :   PRINT
1090 :   PRINT"Resistors with values less than 10 ohm"
1100 :   PRINT"or greater than 99000000000 ohm are not"
1110 :   PRINT"covered by this program"
1120 :   PRINT:PRINT
1130 :   INPUT"Resistance value in ohm";rst
1140 :   rst=INT(rst)
1150 :   IF rst>=10 AND rst<=9.9E+10 THEN flag=0
1160 :   rst$=STR$(rst)
1170 WEND
1180 :
1190 CLS
1200 LOCATE 1,4
1210 PRINT"Enter 1, 2 or 3 depending on whether"
1220 PRINT"the tolerence is 5%, 10% or 20%"
1230 PRINT"respectively."
1240 PRINT
1250 PRINT"All entries other than 1 or 2 will be"
1260 PRINT"assumed to mean 20% tolerance."
1270 PRINT:PRINT
1280 INPUT"Tolerance (1, 2 or 3)";t$
1290 IF t$<>"1" AND t$<>"2" THEN t$="3"
1300 :
1310 CLS
1320 LOCATE 1,4
1330 a(1)=VAL(MID$(rst$,2,1))
1340 a(2)=VAL(MID$(rst$,3,1))
1350 a(3)=LEN(rst$)-3
1360 a(4)=ASC(t$)-39
1370 :
1380 FOR n=1 TO 4
```

```
1390 :   PRINT,"Band";n;"is ";b$(a(n)+1)
1400 NEXT
1410 :
1420 GOSUB 1470:REM Any key
1430 RETURN
1440 :
1450 :
1460 REM Any key
1470 PRINT:PRINT:PRINT
1480 a$="":REM empty string
1490 PRINT TAB(5)"PRESS ANY KEY FOR INSTRUCTIONS"
1500 WHILE LEN(a$)=0:a$=INKEY$:WEND
1510 RETURN
```

P85 Volumes Of Solids

This program calculates the volumes of spheres, cylinders and cones or pyramids.

It could be extended to calculate the volumes of other regular solids.

COMMANDS

Key in the program and RUN.
Follow the instructions.

```
10 REM Volume of solids
20 BORDER 1
30 PAPER 0:INK 0,1
40 PEN 1:INK 1,24
50 MODE 1
60 LOCATE 10,3
70 PRINT"VOLUME OF SOLIDS"
80 PRINT TAB(10)"****************"
90 LOCATE 5,8
100 PRINT TAB(5)"Press Key 1 for sphere"
110 PRINT
120 PRINT TAB(5)"Press Key 2 for cylinder"
130 PRINT
140 PRINT TAB(5)"Press Key 3 for cone or pyramid"
150 PRINT
160 PRINT TAB(5)"Press Key 4 to finish
170 WHILE a$<>"1" AND a$<>"2" AND a$<>"3" AND a$<>"4"
180 :   a$=INKEY$
190 WEND
200 CLS
210 a=VAL(a$)
220 IF a=4 THEN END
230 ON a GOSUB 280,450,690
240 RUN
250 :
260 :
270 REM Sphere
280 PRINT TAB(10)"VOLUME OF A SPHERE"
290 PRINT TAB(10)"******************"
300 rd=-1
310 LOCATE 1,6
320 WHILE rd<0
330 :   INPUT"What is the radius";rd
340 WEND
350 :
360 vl=4*PI*rd*rd*rd/3
370 PRINT:PRINT:PRINT
380 PRINT"The volume of a sphere of radius";rd
390 PRINT
```

```
400 PRINT"is";vl
410 GOSUB 1490
420 RETURN
430 :
440 :
450 REM Cylinder
460 PRINT TAB(10)"VOLUME OF A CYLINDER"
470 PRINT TAB(10)"********************"
480 ht=-1
490 LOCATE 1,6
500 WHILE ht<0
510 :  INPUT"What is the height";ht
520 WEND
530 PRINT:PRINT
540 rd=-1
550 WHILE rd<0
560 :  INPUT"What is the base radius";rd
570 WEND
580 PRINT:PRINT:PRINT
590 PRINT"The volume of a cylinder of base"
600 PRINT
610 PRINT"radius";rd;"and height";ht
620 PRINT
630 PRINT"is";PI*rd*rd*ht
640 GOSUB 1490
650 RETURN
660 :
670 :
680 REM Cone
690 PRINT TAB(11)"VOLUME OF A CONE"
700 PRINT TAB(11)"****************"
710 LOCATE 1,6
720 INPUT"Do you know the base area";y$
730 IF LEFT$(y$,1)="y" OR LEFT$(y$,1)="Y" THEN Y=1 ELSE Y=2
740 ON Y GOSUB 910,1000
750 PRINT
760 ht=-1
770 WHILE ht<0
780 :  INPUT"What is the height";ht
790 WEND
800 PRINT:PRINT
810 PRINT"The volume of a cone of base"
820 PRINT
830 PRINT"area";ar;"and height";ht
840 PRINT
850 PRINT"is";ar*ht/2
860 GOSUB 1490
870 RETURN
880 :
890 :
900 REM Get base area
910 PRINT:PRINT
920 ar=-1
930 WHILE ar<0
940 :  INPUT"What is the area";ar
950 WEND
960 RETURN
```

```
970 :
980 :
990 REM Select base shape
1000 PRINT:PRINT
1010 PRINT"Select base shape by pressing:"
1020 PRINT
1030 PRINT"Key 1 for equilateral triangle"
1040 PRINT"Key 2 for square"
1050 PRINT"Key 3 for circle
1060 PRINT
1070 WHILE c$<>"1" AND c$<>"2" AND c$<>"3"
1080 :  c$=INKEY$
1090 WEND
1100 c=VAL(c$)
1110 ON c GOSUB 1220,1310,1400
1120 :
1130 CLS
1140 PRINT TAB(11)"VOLUME OF A CONE"
1150 PRINT TAB(11)"****************"
1160 LOCATE 1,6
1170 PRINT"Area of base is";ar
1180 RETURN
1190 :
1200 :
1210 REM Triangle
1220 sd=-1
1230 WHILE sd<0
1240 :  INPUT"Length of side of triangle";sd
1250 WEND
1260 ar=0.5*sd*sd*SIN(PI/2)
1270 RETURN
1280 :
1290 :
1300 REM Square
1310 sd=-1
1320 WHILE sd<0
1330 :  INPUT"Length of side of square";sd
1340 WEND
1350 ar=sd*sd
1360 RETURN
1370 :
1380 :
1390 REM Circle
1400 rd=-1
1410 WHILE rd<0
1420 :  INPUT"Radius of circle";rd
1430 WEND
1440 ar=PI*rd*rd
1450 RETURN
1460 :
1470 :
1480 REM Any key
1490 PRINT:PRINT:PRINT
1500 PRINT TAB(8)"PRESS ANY KEY TO RETURN"
1510 WHILE LEN(b$)=0:b$=INKEY$:WEND
1520 RETURN
```

Physics Experiments 1 and 2

The next two programs are an attempt to show how a micro could be used within a physics laboratory to take some of the drudgery out of experimentation.

The programs are based on two experiments in F. Tyler's "A Laboratory Manual of Physics", Edward Arnold, 1966.

COMMANDS

Use WORK SHEETS and programs to perform the experiments.

P86 EXPERIMENT 1 - MOMENT OF INERTIA

Work Sheet 1

Determination of the moment of inertia of a flywheel.

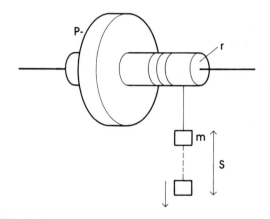

Apparatus

Wall supported flywheel of standard pattern: a   weight   is
attached to a length of fine cord which is wrapped round   the
axle, the free end being passed through a hole in   the   axle.
The length of the cord is adjusted so that the cord   detaches
itself from the axle when   the   weight   reaches   the   ground.
Callipers, stopwatch, metre rule.

Method

The value of m is obtained by weighing; the radius r   of   the
axle is found by using callipers.

The weight (m) is allowed to fall through a measured distance
(s) to the ground, and the time of descent (t) is taken by a
stopwatch.   The number of revolutions (n) of the wheel during
this time   is   taken by observing a mark made on   the
circumference of the wheel at P.   The further revolutions (p)
made by the wheel before coming to rest after m   is   detached
are also counted by reference to the mark P.   The   experiment
is repeated three times for the same distance (s).

Perform the experiment as follows:

Power on microcomputer.
Load program.
Take measurements m, r and s.
RUN the program.
Perform the experiment   as   directed,   and   enter   values   as
prompted.


```
10 REM Moment of inertia
20 PAPER 0:INK 0,24
30 INK 1,1
40 INK 2,6
50 PAPER 0
60 PEN 1
70 BORDER 24
80 MODE 1
90   PRINT TAB(8)"***********************"
100   PRINT TAB(8)"*                     *"
110   PRINT TAB(8)"* PHYSICS EXPERIMENT 1 *"
120   PRINT TAB(8)"*                     *"
130   PRINT TAB(8)"***********************"
```

```
140 PRINT:PRINT:PRINT
150 PEN 2
160 PRINT TAB(11)"----------------"
170 PRINT TAB(11)"MOMENT OF INERTIA"
180 PRINT TAB(17)"OF A"
190 PRINT TAB(15)"FLYWHEEL"
200 PRINT TAB(11)"----------------"
210 PRINT:PRINT:PRINT
220 PEN 1
230 PRINT TAB(9)"Please read Work Sheet."
240 PRINT
250 PEN 2
260 PRINT TAB(7)"Press any key to when ready."
270 a$=INKEY$:IF LEN(a$)=0 THEN 270
280 :
290 y$="y"
300 WHILE LOWER$(y$)="y"
310 :   r=0:m=0:s=0
320 :   CLS
330 :   PEN 1
340 :   INPUT "Radius of axle (cm)";r
350 :   r=r/100
360 :   PRINT
370 :   INPUT "Mass of weight (kg)";m
380 :   PRINT
390 :   INPUT "Distance to ground (cm)";s
400 :   s=s/100
410 :
420 :   tt=0:nn=0:pp=0
430 :   FOR k=1 TO 3
440 :     CLS
450 :     PRINT TAB(10)"PERFORM EXPERIMENT"
460 :     LOCATE 16,5
470 :     PEN 2
480 :     PRINT"RUN";k
490 :     PRINT TAB(16)"*****"
500 :     PRINT:PRINT
510 :     PEN 1
520 :     INPUT "Time (secs)";t
530 :     PRINT
540 :     INPUT "N (revs)";n
550 :     PRINT
560 :     INPUT "P (revs)";p
570 :     tt=tt+t
580 :     nn=nn+n
590 :     pp=pp+p
600 :   NEXT
610 :
620 :   CLS
630 :   g=9.81:REM Acceleration due to gravity
640 :   t=tt/3:n=nn/3:p=pp/3
650 :   ON ERROR GOTO 850
660 :   it=m*r*r*(g*t*t/s-1)*p/(p+n)
670 :
680 :   LOCATE 1,8
690 :   PEN 2
700 :   PRINT"Moment of inertia =";
```

```
710 :   PEN 1
720 :   PRINT USING "####.##";it;
730 :   PEN 2
740 :   PRINT" kg-sq metre."
750 :   PRINT"======================================="
760 :   PRINT:PRINT:PRINT
770 :   PEN 1
780 :   INPUT "Another experiment (y/n)";y$
790 WEND
800 CLS
810 END
820 :
830 :
840 REM Error routine
850 LOCATE 1,10
860 PRINT"Error in data - cannot calculate result."
870 PRINT
880 PEN 2
890 PRINT TAB(5)"Press any key to rerun program."
900 a$=INKEY$:IF LEN(a$)=0 THEN 900
910 RUN
```

Work Sheet 2

Determination of the focal length of a concave mirror.

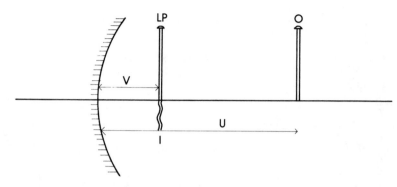

Apparatus

Concave mirror in stand, two retort stands with clamps and pins, metre rule.

Method

The object pin O is placed a given distance (u) from the concave mirror. The position of the image I formed by reflection in the mirror is located by the method of non-parallax using the second pin (locating pin LP). The distance (v) of the locating pin from the mirror is measured. O and I are said to be conjugate points. A series of values of v for a given range of values of u are obtained.

The computer program is used to calculate the focal length of the mirror from each measurement. The average of these values, and their standard deviation, are calculated and presented on the screen.

```
10 REM Focal length
20 PAPER 0:INK 0,24
30 INK 1,1
40 INK 2,6
50 PAPER 0
60 PEN 1
70 BORDER 24
80 MODE 1
90  PRINT TAB(8)"***********************"
100  PRINT TAB(8)"*                     *"
110  PRINT TAB(8)"* PHYSICS EXPERIMENT 2 *"
120  PRINT TAB(8)"*                     *"
130  PRINT TAB(8)"***********************"
140 PRINT:PRINT:PRINT
150 PEN 2
160 PRINT TAB(12)"----------------"
170 PRINT TAB(14)"FOCAL LENGTH"
180 PRINT TAB(18)"OF A"
190 PRINT TAB(13)"CONCAVE MIRROR"
200 PRINT TAB(12)"----------------"
210 PRINT:PRINT:PRINT
220 PEN 1
230 PRINT TAB(9)"Please read Work Sheet."
240 PEN 2
250 LOCATE 8,19
260 INPUT "How many measurements";mea%
270 IF mea%<1 THEN RUN
280 :
290 ON ERROR GOTO 770
300 y$="y"
310 WHILE LOWER$(y$)="y"
320 :   sm=0:ssq=0
330 :   FOR k=1 TO mea%
340 :     CLS
350 :     PEN 1
360 :     PRINT TAB(10)"PERFORM EXPERIMENT"
370 :     LOCATE 13,5
380 :     PEN 2
390 :     PRINT"Measurement";k
400 :     PRINT TAB(13)"************"
410 :     PRINT:PRINT
420 :     PEN 1
430 :     INPUT "U = ",u
440 :     PRINT
450 :     INPUT "V = ",v
460 :     t=1/(1/u+1/v)
470 :     sm=sm+t
480 :     ssq=ssq+t*t
490 :   NEXT
500 :
510 :   CLS
520 :   mn=sm/mea%
530 :   dv=SQR(ssq/mea%-mn*mn)
540 :   LOCATE 6,8
550 :   PEN 2
560 :   PRINT"Average focal length = ";
570 :   PEN 1
```

```
580 :   PRINT USING "####.##";mn
590 :   PEN 2
600 :   PRINT TAB(6)"-----------------------------"
610 :   PRINT:PRINT
620 :   PEN 2
630 :   PRINT TAB(7)"Standard deviation = ";
640 :   PEN 1
650 :   PRINT USING "####.##";dv
660 :   PEN 2
670 :   PRINT TAB(7)"==========================="
680 :   LOCATE 7,17
690 :   PEN 1
700 :   INPUT "Another experiment (y/n)";y$
710 WEND
720 CLS
730 END
740 :
750 :
760 REM Error routine
770 CLS
780 LOCATE 1,10
790 PRINT"Error in data - cannot calculate result."
800 PRINT
810 PEN 2
820 PRINT TAB(5)"Press any key to rerun program."
830 a$=INKEY$:IF LEN(a$)=0 THEN 830
840 RUN
```

P88 Resistors

This program computes the resultant resistance of an electric circuit of the following type:

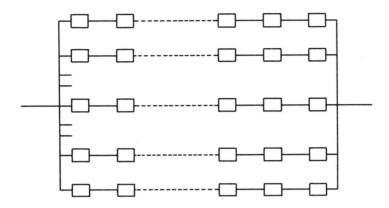

COMMANDS

Key in the program and RUN.
Follow the instructions, entering the   resistance   values   as required.

```
10 REM Resistors
20 PAPER 0:INK 0,1
30 PEN 1:INK 1,24
40 BORDER 1
50 MODE 1
60 LOCATE 15,2
70 PRINT"RESISTORS"
80 LOCATE 1,5
90 PRINT"This program computes the resitance of"
100 PRINT"a circuit comprising several branches"
110 PRINT"connected in parallel, each branch"
120 PRINT"consisting of one or more series"
130 PRINT"resistors."
140 LOCATE 1,15
150 PRINT"PRESS ANY KEY TO CONTINUE"
160 WHILE LEN(a$)=0:a$=INKEY$:WEND
170 :
180 CLS
190 WHILE br%<1
200 :   INPUT"Number of branches";br%
210 WEND
220 :
230 FOR n=1 TO br%
240 :   GOSUB 570:REM Branch number
```

```
250 :
260 :    rs%=-1
270 :    WHILE rs%<1
280 :      INPUT"Number of resistors";rs%
290 :    WEND
300 :
310 :    FOR k=1 TO rs%
320 :      GOSUB 570:REM Branch number
330 :      vl=-1
340 :      WHILE vl<0
350 :        PRINT"Value of resistor";k;
360 :        INPUT vl
370 :      WEND
380 :      R(n)=R(n)+vl
390 :    NEXT
400 :    IF R(n)=0 THEN zer=1:n=br% ELSE cn=cn+1/R(n)
410 NEXT
420 :
430 IF zer=1 THEN ttl=0 ELSE ttl=1/cn
440 CLS
450 LOCATE 9,9
460 PRINT"Total resistance is"
470 LOCATE 8,11
480 PRINT ttl;"ohm"
490 LOCATE 9,22
500 INPUT"Another circuit (Y/N)";y$
510 IF LEFT$(y$,1)="Y" OR LEFT$(y$,1)="y" THEN RUN
520 CLS
530 END
540 :
550 :
560 REM Print branch number
570 CLS
580 LOCATE 15,3
590 PRINT"BRANCH";n
600 LOCATE 1,6
610 RETURN
```

P89 Calculator

There are many occasions when you need the capability of a simple calculator rather than a complex computer. This program simulates a simple four function (+,-,*,/) calculator.

The program could be expanded to provide memory-add, memory-subtract and memory-read features.

COMMANDS

Key in the program and RUN.
Use the numeric keys and +, -, * and / to perform arithmetic.
Use '.' for decimal point and '=' to get final answer. Use the C, A, and S keys as instructed.

```
10 REM Calculator
20 PAPER 0:INK 0,0
30 PEN 1:INK 1,23
40 BORDER 0
50 MODE 0
60 PRINT TAB(6)"**********"
70 PRINT TAB(6)"CALCULATOR"
80 PRINT TAB(6)"**********"
90 PRINT:PRINT
100 PRINT"Key C clear current"
110 PRINT TAB(7)"entry."
120 PRINT
130 PRINT"Key A clear all"
140 PRINT TAB(7)"entries."
150 PRINT
160 PRINT"Key S stop program.
170 e$="":REM no space
180 ON ERROR GOTO 680
190 :
200 WHILE b$<>"s"
210 :   b$=INKEY$:IF b$=e$ THEN 210
220 :   b$=LOWER$(b$)
230 :   aa=ASC(b$)
240 :   IF (aa>47 AND aa<58) OR b$="." THEN GOSUB 340
250 :   IF b$="+" OR b$="-" OR b$="*" THEN GOSUB 450
260 :   IF b$="/" OR b$="=" THEN GOSUB 450
270 :   IF b$="a" OR b$="c" THEN GOSUB 600
280 WEND
290 MODE 1
300 END
310 :
320 :
330 REM Number or decimal point
340 IF f$="=" THEN a$=e$:f$=e$:r=0
350 a$=a$+b$
```

```
360 IF LEN(a$)>8 THEN a$=LEFT$(a$,8)
370 LOCATE 1,17
380 PRINT SPACE$(12)
390 LOCATE 1,17
400 PRINT TAB (9-LEN(a$));a$
410 RETURN
420 :
430 :
440 REM Operator
450 IF f$="+" OR f$=e$ THEN r=r+VAL(a$)
460 IF f$="-" THEN r=r-VAL(a$)
470 IF f$="*" THEN r=r*VAL(a$)
480 IF f$="/" THEN r=r/VAL(a$)
490 f$=b$
500 IF f$="=" THEN p$=CHR$(32) ELSE p$=f$
510 LOCATE 1,17
520 PRINT SPACE$(20)
530 LOCATE 1,17
540 PRINT TAB(9-LEN(STR$(r)));r;TAB(16);p$
550 a$=e$
560 RETURN
570 :
580 :
590 REM Clear
600 LOCATE 1,17
610 IF b$="a" THEN sp=20:f$=e$:r=0 ELSE sp=12
620 PRINT SPACE$(sp)
630 a$=e$
640 RETURN
650 :
660 :
670 REM Error routine
680 LOCATE 1,17
690 PRINT SPACE$(20)
700 LOCATE 1,17
710 PRINT "ERROR"
720 PRINT
730 PRINT "Press any key."
740 b$=INKEY$:IF b$=e$ THEN 740
750 RUN
```

P90   Coordinate Conversion

It can happen quite often that you have points plotted on a
graph in the rectangular (x,y) format and wish to convert the
co-ordinates of these points to the polar (r,θ) format, or
vice versa, as in the following figure:

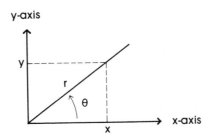

The conversion formulae are:

    x=r*COS(θ)
    y=r*SIN(θ)
    r=x^2+y^2
    θ=ARC TAN(y/x)

This is a demonstration program and the formulae used are
accurate only for the first quadrant. The special case when
x=0 has not been dealt with, nor has any 'trap' been set for
entry of negative values of r.   The program, extended to
incorporate all these features, could be a valuable tool for
mathematicians.

COMMANDS

Key in the program and RUN.
Follow the instructions.


```
10 REM Coordinate conversion
20 INK 0,24
30 INK 1,1
40 PAPER 0
50 PEN 1
60 BORDER 24
70 MODE 1
80 PRINT TAB(14)"------------"
90 PRINT TAB(15)"COORDINATE"
100 PRINT TAB(15)"CONVERSION"
110 PRINT TAB(14)"------------"
```

```
120 GOSUB 730:REM Angle units
130 ON ERROR GOTO 1010
140 :
150 REM Menu
160 WHILE c%<>3
170 :   c%=0
180 :   CLS
190 :   LOCATE 6,6
200 :   PRINT"Key 1. Rectangular to polar"
210 PRINT
220 :   PRINT TAB(6)"Key 2. Polar to rectangular"
230 PRINT
240 :   PRINT TAB(6)"Key 3. Stops program"
250 :   PRINT:PRINT
260 :   PRINT TAB(4)"What is your choice - 1, 2 or 3?"
270 :   WHILE c%<1 OR c%>3
280 :     c$=INKEY$:IF c$="" THEN 280
290 :     c%=ASC(c$)-48
300 :   WEND
310 :   ON c% GOSUB 400,560
320 WEND
330 CLS
340 END
350 :
360 :
370 :
380 :
390 REM Rectangular to polar
400 CLS
410 INPUT "What is x-coordinate";x
420 PRINT
430 INPUT "What is y-coordinate";y
440 r=SQR(x*x*y*y)
450 a=ATN(y/x)
460 CLS
470 PRINT:PRINT:PRINT
480 PRINT TAB(6)"Radial value =";r
490 PRINT
500 PRINT TAB(6)"Angle =";FNa1(a);t$
510 GOSUB 910
520 RETURN
530 :
540 :
550 REM Polar to rectangular
560 CLS
570 INPUT "What is radial value";r
580 PRINT
590 INPUT "What is angle";a
600 a=FNa2(a)
610 x=r*COS(a)
620 y=r*SIN(a)
630 CLS
640 PRINT:PRINT:PRINT
650 PRINT TAB(6)"X-coordinate =";x
660 PRINT
670 PRINT TAB(6)"Y-coordinate =";y
680 GOSUB 910
```

```
690 RETURN
700 :
710 :
720 REM Angle units
730 PRINT:PRINT:PRINT:PRINT
740 PRINT TAB(6)"Do you wish angles to be in:"
750 PRINT
760 PRINT TAB(14)"1 - radians"
770 PRINT TAB(14)"2 - degrees"
780 PRINT
790 an%=0
800 PRINT TAB(6)"What is your choice (1 or 2)?"
810 WHILE an%<1 OR an%>2
820 :   a$=INKEY$:IF a$="" THEN 820
830 :   an%=ASC(a$)-48
840 WEND
850 t$="degrees":DEF FNa1(a)=a*180/PI:DEF FNa2(a)=a*PI/180
860 IF an%=1 THEN t$="radians":DEF FNa1(a)=a:DEF FNa2(a)=a
870 RETURN
880 :
890 :
900 REM Return to menu
910 PRINT:PRINT:PRINT
920 PRINT TAB(6)"Press any key to continue"
930 b$=INKEY$:IF b$="" THEN 930
940 LOCATE 6,15
950 INPUT "Want to alter angle units (y/n)";y$
960 IF LEFT$(LOWER$(y$),1)="y" THEN CLS:GOSUB 730
970 RETURN
980 :
990 :
1000 REM Error routine
1010 CLS
1020 PRINT"Conversion  cannot  be calculated  from"
1030 PRINT"data entered."
1040 PRINT
1050 PRINT
1060 PRINT"Press any key to run program again."
1070 a$=INKEY$:IF a$="" THEN 1070
1080 RUN
```

P91 Vector Multiplication

This is a rather simple program which can be used to find the dot and cross products of vectors. The vectors used have only three components.

The program would have been more complex if it had been written for general vectors. We believe, however, that this is a useful routine to have in any program library.

COMMANDS

Key in the program and RUN.
Enter vectors when prompted.


```
10 REM Vector multiplication
20 INK 0,1
30 INK 1,24
40 PAPER 0
50 PEN 1
60 BORDER 1
70 MODE 1
80 PRINT TAB(10)"VECTOR MULTIPLICATION"
90 PRINT TAB(10)"*********************"
100 PRINT:PRINT:PRINT
110 PRINT"This program computes the dot and cross"
120 PRINT"products of two vectors."
130 PRINT
140 PRINT"The vectors are entered in component"
150 PRINT"form and their products are then given."
160 PRINT
170 PRINT"The vectors must be in 3-D space."
180 PRINT:PRINT:PRINT
190 PRINT"Press any key to continue."
200 a$=INKEY$:IF a$="" THEN 200
210 :
220 y$="y"
230 WHILE LEFT$(LOWER$(y$),1)="y"
240 :    CLS
250 :    PRINT"Enter components of first vector:"
260 :    PRINT:PRINT:PRINT
270 :    FOR n=0 TO 2
280 :      PRINT"Component ";STR$(n+1);
290 :      INPUT U(n)
300 :      PRINT
310 :    NEXT
320 :
330 :    CLS
340 :    PRINT"Enter components of second vector:"
350 :    PRINT:PRINT:PRINT
360 :    FOR n=0 TO 2
370 :      PRINT"Component";n+1;
```

```
380 :    INPUT V(n)
390 :      PRINT
400 : NEXT
410 :
420 : REM Dot product
430 : d=0
440 : FOR n=0 TO 2
450 :    d=d+U(n)*V(n)
460 : NEXT
470 :
480 : REM Cross product
490 : w(0)=U(1)*V(2)-U(2)*V(1)
500 : w(1)=U(2)*V(0)-U(0)*V(2)
510 : w(2)=U(0)*V(1)-U(1)*V(0)
520 :
530 : CLS
540 : PRINT TAB(14)"CROSS PRODUCT"
550 : PRINT TAB(14)"*************"
560 : PRINT:PRINT
570 : PRINT SPC(4)"Vector 1";SPC(4);"Vector 2"SPC(5)"Product"
580 : PRINT SPC(4)"--------"SPC(4)"--------"SPC(5)"-------"
590 : FOR n=0 TO 2
600 :    PRINT USING "#########.##";U(n);V(n);w(n)
610 : NEXT
620 :
630 : PRINT:PRINT:PRINT:PRINT
640 : PRINT TAB(15)"DOT PRODUCT"
650 : PRINT TAB(15)"***********"
660 : PRINT:PRINT
670 : PRINT TAB(8)"Dot product is";INT(100*d+0.5)/100
680 : PRINT:PRINT:PRINT
690 : INPUT "Do you wish another product (y/n)";y$
700 WEND
710 CLS
720 END
```

P92 Quadratic Equations

In this program we have to solve:

$$Ax^2 + Bx + C = 0 \qquad\qquad (I)$$

To do this we use the formula:

$$x = (-B \pm SQR(B*B - 4*A*C))/2/A \qquad\qquad (II)$$

This gives the two roots of (I). There **are**, however, some problems:

1. If A=0 we have division by zero in equation (II).
    In this case the solution is x = C/B.

2. If B*B - 4*A*C = 0 we have only one root.
    In this case the solution is x = -B/(2*A).

3. If B*B - 4*A*C < 0 we have complex roots.

COMMANDS

Key in the program and RUN.
Enter the coefficients in the correct order when prompted.


```
10 REM Quadratic equations
20 INK 0,1
30 INK 1,24
40 PAPER 0
50 PEN 1
60 BORDER 1
70 MODE 1
80 PRINT TAB(11)"QUADRATIC EQUATIONS"
90 PRINT TAB(11)"*******************"
100 PRINT:PRINT
110 PRINT"This program  solves  equations  of the"
120 PRINT"form:"
130 PRINT
140 PRINT TAB(14)"a*x^2+b*x+c=0"
150 PRINT:PRINT
160 PRINT"Enter  the  three  coefficients  in the"
170 PRINT"correct order."
180 PRINT:PRINT
190 INPUT "Coefficient of x^2 (a)=";a
200 INPUT "Coefficient of x   (b)=";b
210 INPUT "Constant term      (c)=";c
220 IF a=0 AND b=0 THEN RUN:REM Not a sensible condition
230 :
```

```
240 IF a<>0 THEN a$=STR$(a)+"*x^2"
250 IF b>0 THEN b$=MID$(STR$(b),2)+"*x"
260 IF a<>0 AND b>0 THEN b$="+"+b$
270 IF c>0 THEN c$="+"+MID$(STR$(c),2)
280 IF c<0 THEN c$=STR$(c)
290 e$=a$+b$+c$+"=0"
300 PRINT
310 PRINT"Equation is ";e$
320 PRINT
330 INPUT "Is this correct (y/n)";y$
340 IF LEFT$(LOWER$(y$),1)<>"y" THEN RUN
350 :
360 CLS
370 t=INT((28-LEN(e$))/2)
380 PRINT TAB(t)"Equation is ";e$
390 PRINT:PRINT
400 IF a=0 THEN PRINT TAB(6)"The solution is: x =";-c/b:f=1
410 WHILE f=0
420 :   d=b*b-4*a*c:REM Discriminant
430 :   IF d=0 THEN GOSUB 570
440 :   IF d>0 THEN GOSUB 640
450 :   IF d<0 THEN GOSUB 730
460 :   f=1
470 WEND
480 :
490 PRINT:PRINT:PRINT
500 INPUT "Do you wish to solve another (y/n)";y$
510 IF LEFT$(LOWER$(y$),1)="y" THEN RUN
520 CLS
530 END
540 :
550 :
560 REM Equal roots
570 PRINT TAB(t)"We have equal roots."
580 PRINT:PRINT
590 PRINT TAB(6)"The solution is: x =";-b/2/a
600 RETURN
610 :
620 :
630 REM Real roots
640 PRINT TAB(t)"We have two real roots."
650 PRINT:PRINT
660 PRINT TAB(6)"Root 1 is: x =";(-b+SQR(d))/2/a
670 PRINT
680 PRINT TAB(6)"Root 2 is: x =";(-b-SQR(d))/2/a
690 RETURN
700 :
710 :
720 REM Complex roots
730 PRINT TAB(t)"We have complex roots."
740 PRINT:PRINT
750 PRINT TAB(6)"Root 1 is: x =";-b/2/a;"+"
760 PRINT TAB(21);"i*(";SQR(-d)/2/a;")"
770 PRINT
780 PRINT TAB(6)"Root 2 is: x =";-b/2/a;"-"
790 PRINT TAB(21);"i*(";SQR(-d)/2/a;")"
800 RETURN
```

P93 Factorization

This program finds the prime factors of positive integers. Any positive integer N may be expressed in terms of prime numbers and indices. The index of a prime number is the power to which that number is raised in the factorization of N.

For example:

$$180 = 2^2 * 3^2 * 5$$

We use a method of repeated division to find the set of factors for N.

Let us consider an example - find the prime factors of 180.

The first possible factor of 180 is 2, and we can write:

    180 = 2*90 = 2*2*45

Thus 2 is a factor of 180 and of 90, but it is not a factor of 45. That is to say that dividing 45 by two gives a remainder which is not zero.

We can now try 3:

    180 = 2*2*3*15 = 2*2*3*3*5

Trying the next prime, 5, gives a result on division of 1. This indicates that all the factors have been found.

Thus:

    180 = 2*2*3*3*5*1 = 2^2 * 3^3 * 5

The program presented here uses this algorithm.

COMMANDS

Key in the program and RUN.
Enter the number to be factorized.


```
10 REM Factorization
20 INK 0,1
30 INK 1,24
40 PAPER 0
50 PEN 1
60 BORDER 1
70 MODE 1
80 PRINT TAB(14)"FACTORIZATION"
```

```
 90 PRINT TAB(14)"*************"
100 PRINT:PRINT
110 PRINT"This  program  is  used  to  factorize a"
120 PRINT"a positive  integer into prime factors."
130 PRINT
140 PRINT"In its  present  form the  program uses"
150 PRINT"only the primes less than 100."
160 PRINT:PRINT:PRINT
170 INPUT "Number to be factorized";num
180 num=INT(num)
190 IF num<2 THEN RUN:REM Trivial entries ignored
200 q=num
210 d=100:REM Change this line to alter program's range
220 DIM f(d),i(d)
230 :
240 REM Find indices
250 FOR k=2 TO d
260 :   t=q-INT(q/k)*k
270 :   WHILE t=0
280 :      f(k)=1
290 :      i(k)=i(k)+1
300 :      q=INT(q/k)
310 :      t=q-INT(q/k)*k
320 :   WEND
330 NEXT
340 :
350 REM If there is a 1 in the kth position of the factor
360 REM array then k is a factor and i(k) is the index
370 REM of that factor.
380 :
390 REM The next section of code prints the factorization.
400 REM The first 1 is printed to tidy up the display,
410 REM even though 1 might not be considered a prime.
420 :
430 CLS
440 c=1
450 a$="1"
460 FOR k=2 TO d
470 :   b$="  *"+STR$(k)+"^"+MID$(STR$(i(k)),2)
480 :   IF f(k)=1 THEN a$=a$+b$:c=c*k^i(k)
490 NEXT
500 :
510 IF c>=num THEN GOSUB 600 ELSE GOSUB 710
520 PRINT:PRINT
530 INPUT "Do you wish another run (y/n)";y$
540 IF LEFT$(LOWER$(y$),1)="y" THEN RUN
550 CLS
560 END
570 :
580 :
590 REM Factorization OK
600 PRINT TAB(5)"The prime factorization of:"
610 PRINT
620 PRINT TAB(4);num
630 PRINT
640 PRINT TAB(5)"is"
650 PRINT
```

```
660 PRINT TAB(5);a$
670 RETURN
680 :
690 :
700 REM Factorization incorrect
710 PRINT"Either the  number has  a prime  factor"
720 PRINT"greater   than  100,  or  the  rounding"
730 PRINT"errors of  the micro  have  muddled the"
740 PRINT"calculation."
750 RETURN
```

P94 **Factorial**

In statistics we frequently wish to calculate objects of the form:

    N * (N-1) * (N-2) * ...... * 3 * 2 * 1

For example, if we want to know the number of ways of arranging the letters in the word COMPUTER, then:

    We have 8 ways of choosing the first letter;
    We have 7 ways of choosing the second letter;
    We have 6 ways of choosing the third letter;

and so on.

Thus in total we have:

    8 * 7 * 6 * 5 * 4 * 3 * 2 * 1 = 40320

ways of arranging the letters of the word COMPUTER.

Such objects are known as factorials, and are defined as follows:

    N! = N * (N-1) * (N-2) * ..... * 3 * 2 * 1

Where ! is the symbol for factorial.

COMMANDS

Key in the program and RUN.
Follow the instructions.


```
10 REM Factorial
20 INK 0,1
30 INK 1,24
40 PAPER 0
50 PEN 1
60 BORDER 1
70 MODE 1
80 PRINT TAB(16)"FACTORIAL"
90 PRINT TAB(16)"---------"
100 PRINT:PRINT
110 PRINT"This program is used to evaluate the"
120 PRINT"factorial of a positive integer less"
130 PRINT"than or equal to 33."
140 PRINT
150 PRINT"The program uses the formula:"
160 PRINT
170 PRINT"n!=n*(n-1)*(n-2)*(n-3)*....*3*2*1."
```

```
180 PRINT
190 PRINT"The limitation of 33 is   because of the"
200 PRINT"limited range  of numbers   which can be"
210 PRINT"held inside a computer."
220 PRINT:PRINT:PRINT
230 INPUT "Please enter number (1 to 33) ",n%
240 IF n%<1 OR n%>33 THEN RUN
250 :
260 CLS
270 f=1
280 FOR k=1 TO n%
290 :   f=f*k
300 NEXT
310 PRINT:PRINT:PRINT
320 PRINT TAB(8)"The factorial of";n%;"is"
330 PRINT
340 PRINT TAB(7);f
350 PRINT TAB(8)"-";
360 FOR k=3 TO LEN(STR$(f))
370 :   PRINT"-";
380 NEXT
390 PRINT:PRINT:PRINT
400 INPUT "Do you wish another number (y/n)";y$
410 IF LEFT$(LOWER$(y$),1)="y" THEN RUN
420 CLS
430 END
```

P95 Greatest Common Divisor

This program uses the Euclidian Algorithm to compute the greatest common divisor of two natural numbers.

COMMANDS

Key in the program and RUN.
Enter numbers as positive integers.

```
10 REM Greatest common divisor
20 INK 0,1
30 INK 1,24
40 PAPER 0
50 PEN 1
60 BORDER 1
70 MODE 1
80 PRINT TAB(9)"GREATEST COMMON DIVISOR"
90 PRINT TAB(9)"***********************"
100 PRINT:PRINT
110 PRINT"This    program   uses    the   Euclidian"
120 PRINT"algorithm   to   compute   the   greatest"
130 PRINT"common divisor of two natural numbers."
140 PRINT:PRINT
150 INPUT "First number";x1
160 PRINT
170 INPUT "Second number";x2
180 :
190 CLS
200 x1=INT(ABS(x1))
210 a=x1
220 x2=INT(ABS(x2))
230 b=x2
240 ON ERROR GOTO 520
250 IF a<b THEN t=b:b=a:a=t:REM a is larger number
260 :
270 REM The following is the Euclidian algorithm
280 r=1
290 WHILE r<>0
300 :   r=a-(INT(a/b))*b:REM Remainder
310 :   q=INT(a/b):REM Quotient
320 :   a=b
330 :   b=r
340 WEND
350 :
360 PRINT:PRINT:PRINT
370 PRINT TAB(3)"The greatest common divisor of"
380 PRINT
390 PRINT TAB(2);x1;"and"
400 PRINT
410 PRINT TAB(2);x2;"is"
420 PRINT
```

```
430 PRINT TAB(2);a
440 PRINT:PRINT:PRINT
450 INPUT "Do you wish another run (y/n)";y$
460 IF LEFT$(LOWER$(y$),1)="y" THEN RUN
470 CLS
480 END
490 :
500 :
510 REM Error routine
520 PRINT"Calculation cannot be carried out on"
530 PRINT"data entered."
540 PRINT
550 PRINT"Press any key to re-run program."
560 a$=INKEY$:IF a$="" THEN 560
570 RUN
```

P96 Polynomial Multiplication

This program allows the user to multiply two polynomials together.

EXAMPLE

Multiply $(2*x*x + 3*x + 2)$ by $(x + 1)$

If this has to be done by hand we proceed as follows:

$$
\begin{array}{r}
2x^2 + 3x + 2 \\
x + 1 \\
\hline
2x^2 + 3x + 2 \\
2x^3 + 3x^2 + 2x \\
\hline
2x^3 + 5x^2 + 5x + 2 \\
\hline
\end{array}
$$

This can be a rather time consuming exercise when the polynomials become large. This program takes all the work out of it.

The Amstrad, in common with most other micros, cannot express polynomials in a very satisfactory manner, but bear with this and the algorithm can be very useful.

COMMANDS

Key in the program and RUN.
Follow instructions, keying in the parameters as prompted.

```
10 REM Polynomial multiplication
20 INK 0,1
30 INK 1,24
40 PAPER 0
50 PEN 1
60 BORDER 1
70 MODE 1
80 PRINT TAB(8)"POLYNOMIAL MULTIPLICATION"
90 PRINT TAB(8)"************************"
100 PRINT:PRINT
110 PRINT"This program is used to find the result"
120 PRINT"of multiplying two polynomials together."
130 PRINT"The polynomials are of the form:"
140 PRINT
150 PRINT"p(x)=a(m)*x^m+a(m-1)*x^(m-1)+....+a(1)*x+a(0)"
160 PRINT
170 PRINT"q(x)=b(n)*x^n+b(n-1)*x^(n-1)+....+b(1)*x+b(0)"
```

```
180 PRINT
190 PRINT"and the result is:"
200 PRINT
210 PRINT"p(x)*q(x)=c(m+n)*x^(m+n)+c(m+n-1)*x^(m+n-1)....+c(0)
220 PRINT
230 PRINT"You are  required  to enter  the degree"
240 PRINT"and the coefficients of each polynomial."
250 PRINT
260 PRINT"Press any key to continue."
270 a$=INKEY$:IF a$="" THEN 270
280 :
290 DIM a(50),b(50),c(100)
300 REM Polynomials of degree>50 not accepted
310 :
320 m%=-1
330 WHILE m%<0 OR m%>51
340 :  CLS
350 :  INPUT "What is degree of first polynomial";m%
360 WEND
370 :
380 PRINT
390 FOR k=0 TO m%
400 :  PRINT"Coefficient";k;
410 :  INPUT a(k)
420 NEXT
430 :
440 n%=-1
450 WHILE n%<0 OR n%>51
460 :  CLS
470 :  INPUT "What is degree of second polynomial";n%
480 PRINT
490 WEND
500 :
510 FOR k=0 TO n%
520 :  PRINT"Coefficient";k;
530 :  INPUT b(k)
540 NEXT
550 :
560 CLS
570 ON ERROR GOTO 970
580 FOR j=0 TO m%
590 :  FOR k=0 TO n%
600 :    c(k+j)=c(k+j)+b(k)*a(j)
610 :  NEXT
620 NEXT
630 :
640 PRINT"The result of multiplying"
650 PRINT
660 FOR j=m% TO 0 STEP -1
670 :  PRINT a(j);"*x^";j;"+";
680 NEXT
690 PRINT CHR$(8);CHR$(32):REM Delete last +
700 :
710 PRINT
720 PRINT"by"
730 PRINT
740 :
```

```
750 FOR j=n% TO 0 STEP -1
760 :   PRINT b(j);"*x^";j;"+";
770 NEXT
780 PRINT CHR$(8);CHR$(32):REM Delete last +
790 :
800 PRINT
810 PRINT"is"
820 PRINT
830 :
840 FOR j=n%+m% TO 0 STEP -1
850 :   PRINT c(j);"*x^";j;"+";
860 NEXT
870 PRINT CHR$(8);CHR$(32):REM Delete last +
880 :
890 PRINT:PRINT
900 INPUT "Another run (y/n)";y$
910 IF LEFT$(LOWER$(y$),1)="y" THEN RUN
920 CLS
930 END
940 :
950 :
960 REM Error routine
970 PRINT"Calculation  beyond  the  range  of the"
980 PRINT"computer."
990 PRINT:PRINT
1000 PRINT"Press any key to re-run program."
1010 a$=INKEY$:IF a$="" THEN 1010
1020 RUN
```

P97 Secant Method

This program can be used to find a root of a function of a single variable. The secant method can be interpreted geometrically as follows:

Consider the diagram:

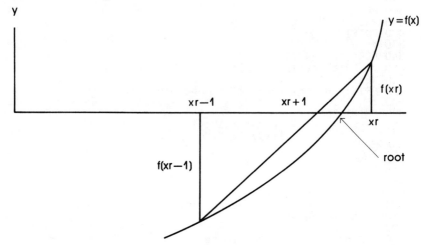

If xr and xr-1 lie on either side of a root we can draw the secant between the points (xr-1,f(xr-1)) and (xr,f(xr)). The secant cuts the x-axis at the point xr+1. Let xr+1 be the new approximation.

Then by similar triangles:

$$\frac{x_{r+1} - x_{r-1}}{-f(x_{r-1})} = \frac{x_r - x_{r+1}}{f(x_r)}$$

$$\therefore \quad x_{r+1} = x_r - f(x_r) \frac{(x_r - x_{r-1})}{f(x_r) - f(x_{r-1})}$$

The same relationship can   be   formed   even   if   both
approximations lie on the same side of the root.

COMMANDS

Key in the program and RUN.
Enter function and initial approximations when required.
Enter accuracy when prompted.

```
10 REM Secant method
20 INK 0,1
30 INK 1,24
40 PAPER 0
50 PEN 1
60 BORDER 1
70 MODE 1
80 PRINT TAB(14)"SECANT METHOD"
90 PRINT TAB(14)"*************"
100 PRINT:PRINT
110 PRINT"This program uses the  secant method to"
120 PRINT"find the root of an equation."
130 PRINT
140 PRINT"Note  that  the method  will attempt to"
150 PRINT"find a root within an  interval even if"
160 PRINT"no root exists."
170 PRINT
180 PRINT"You are required to enter the function,"
190 PRINT"the range of x values  within which the"
200 PRINT"root lies and the required accuracy."
210 PRINT:PRINT
220 PRINT"Press any key to continue."
230 a$=INKEY$:IF a$="" THEN 230
240 :
250 CLS
260 PRINT"To enter the function please type in:"
270 PRINT
280 PRINT"400 def fna(x)="
290 PRINT
300 PRINT"followed directly by the function,"
310 PRINT"then press the ENTER key.  When you"
320 PRINT"have done this, type in:"
330 PRINT
340 PRINT"run 400"
350 PRINT
360 PRINT"and then press the ENTER key again."
```

```
370 PRINT:PRINT:PRINT
380 STOP
390 :
400 REM This line is replaced by the function entered.
410 :
420 CLS
430 ON ERROR GOTO 860
440 INPUT "First point -  x=";p1
450 PRINT
460 INPUT "Second point - x=";p2
470 PRINT
480 INPUT "Accuracy";ac
490 PRINT:PRINT
500 :
510 FOR r=1 TO 40
520 :   f1=FNa(p1)
530 :   f2=FNa(p2)
540 :   p3=p2-f2*(p2-p1)/(f2-f1)
550 :   p1=p2
560 :   p2=p3
570 :   IF ABS(p2-p1)<=ABS(ac) THEN GOSUB 690:f=1:r=40
580 NEXT
590 IF f=0 THEN GOSUB 760
600 :
610 PRINT:PRINT
620 INPUT "Another run (y/n)";y$
630 IF LEFT$(LOWER$(y$),1)="y" THEN RUN
640 CLS
650 END
660 :
670 :
680 REM Root found
690 PRINT"Root is";p2
700 PRINT
710 PRINT"at iteration number";r
720 RETURN
730 :
740 :
750 REM Root not found
760 PRINT"Root not found after 40 iterations."
770 PRINT
780 PRINT"If any root exists near the range"
790 PRINT"entered it lies between:"
800 PRINT
810 PRINT p1;" and ";p2
820 RETURN
830 :
840 :
850 REM Error routine
860 PRINT"Calculation cannot be performed on data"
870 PRINT"given."
880 PRINT
890 PRINT"Press any key to re-run program."
900 a$=INKEY$:IF a$="" THEN 900
910 RUN
```

P98 Method Of Bisections

The method of bisections is based on the use of sign changes to find a root of a function.

Consider the following diagram:

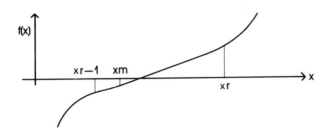

If we have two points, xr and xr-1, such that f(xr) and f(xr-1) have different signs, then there is a root between xr and xr-1. We then evaluate the function at the mid point, xm, between xr and xr-1. If xm=0 then we have a root. If SGN(f(xm)) does not equal SGN(f(xr-1)) then the root lies between xm and xr-1. Otherwise the root lies between xm and xr.

That is the idea behind the method of bisections, which is used in this program.

COMMANDS

Key in the program and RUN.
Enter the function and the end points of the interval straddling the root when prompted.
Enter the accuracy desired.

```
10 REM Method of bisections
20 INK 0,1
30 INK 1,24
40 PAPER 0
50 PEN 1
60 BORDER 1
70 MODE 1
80 PRINT TAB(10)"METHOD OF BISECTIONS"
90 PRINT TAB(10)"********************"
100 PRINT:PRINT
110 PRINT"This   program   uses   the   method  of"
120 PRINT"bisections   to   find   the   root   of   an"
130 PRINT"equation."
```

```
140 PRINT
150 PRINT"Note  that   the method  will attempt to"
160 PRINT"find a root within an  interval even if"
170 PRINT"no root exists."
180 PRINT
190 PRINT"You are required to enter the function,"
200 PRINT"the range of x values  within which the"
210 PRINT"root lies and the required accuracy."
220 PRINT:PRINT
230 PRINT"Press any key to continue."
240 a$=INKEY$:IF a$="" THEN 240
250 :
260 CLS
270 PRINT"To enter the function please type in:"
280 PRINT
290 PRINT"410 def fna(x)="
300 PRINT
310 PRINT"followed directly by the function,"
320 PRINT"then press the ENTER key.  When you"
330 PRINT"have done this, type in:"
340 PRINT
350 PRINT"run 410"
360 PRINT
370 PRINT"and then press the ENTER key again."
380 PRINT:PRINT:PRINT
390 STOP
400 :
410 REM This line is replaced by the function entered.
420 :
430 CLS
440 ON ERROR GOTO 850
450 INPUT "First point -  x=";p1
460 PRINT
470 INPUT "Second point - x=";p2
480 PRINT
490 INPUT "Accuracy";ac
500 PRINT:PRINT
510 :
520 a=1/(p1-p2)
530 FOR r=1 TO 40
540 :  t=(p1+p2)/2:k=p1
550 :  IF SGN(FNa(t))=SGN(FNa(k)) THEN p1=t:ELSE p2=t
560 :  IF FNa(t)=0 THEN PRINT"Solution is";t:r=40:s=3 ELSE s=0
570 :  WHILE s=0
580 :     IF SGN(FNa(p1))=SGN(FNa(p2)) THEN fg=1 ELSE fg=0
590 :     IF ABS(p1-p2)<=ABS(ac) AND fg=0 THEN s=1:r=40
600 :     IF s=0 THEN s=2
610 :  WEND
620 NEXT
630 ON s GOSUB 730,780
640 :
650 PRINT:PRINT
660 INPUT "Another run (y/n)";y$
670 IF LEFT$(LOWER$(y$),1)="y" THEN RUN
680 CLS
690 END
700 :
```

```
710 :
720 REM Root found
730 PRINT"Root lies between:
740 PRINT
750 PRINT p1;" and ";p2
760 RETURN
770 :
780 :
790 REM Root not found
800 PRINT"Root not found after 40 iterations."
810 RETURN
820 :
830 :
840 REM Error routine
850 PRINT"Calculation cannot be performed on data"
860 PRINT"given."
870 PRINT
880 PRINT"Press any key to re-run program."
890 a$=INKEY$:IF a$="" THEN 890
900 RUN
```

P99 Trapezoidal Rule

This program uses the trapezoidal rule to evaluate a definite integral of the form:

$$I = \int_a^b f(x)dx$$

Thus the program requires as input:

f(x)
a and b

A definite integral can be considered to be the area under the graph of a function. The trapezium rule approximates this area by a series of trapeziums, as in the following diagram:

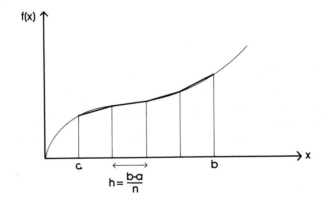

COMMANDS

Key in the program and RUN.
Follow the instructions.


```
10 REM Trapezoidal rule
20 INK 0,1
30 INK 1,24
40 PAPER 0
50 PEN 1
60 BORDER 1
70 MODE 1
80 PRINT TAB(12)"TRAPEZOIDAL RULE"
90 PRINT TAB(12)"++++++++++++++++"
100 PRINT:PRINT
110 PRINT"This program uses  the trapezoidal rule"
120 PRINT"to evaluate a definite integral"
130 PRINT
140 PRINT "You are required to enter:"
150 PRINT
160 PRINT TAB(4)"1. Your function of x."
170 PRINT
180 PRINT TAB(4)"2. The range of values of x over"
190 PRINT TAB(7)"which you wish to value the"
200 PRINT TAB(7)"integral."
210 PRINT
220 PRINT TAB(4)"3. The number of sub-intervals."
230 PRINT:PRINT
240 PRINT"Press any key to continue."
250 a$=INKEY$:IF a$="" THEN 250
260 :
270 CLS
280 PRINT"To enter the function please type in:"
290 PRINT
300 PRINT"420 def fna(x)="
310 PRINT
320 PRINT"followed directly by the function,"
330 PRINT"then press the ENTER key.  When you"
340 PRINT"have done this, type in:"
350 PRINT
360 PRINT"run 420"
370 PRINT
380 PRINT"and then press the ENTER key again."
390 PRINT:PRINT:PRINT
```

```
400 STOP
410 :
420 REM This line is replaced by the function entered.
430 :
440 CLS
450 ON ERROR GOTO 900
460 INPUT "Lower value of x-range";a
470 PRINT
480 INPUT "Upper value of x-range";b
490 PRINT
500 INPUT "Number of points";n%
510 IF n%<2 THEN n%=2
520 IF a>b THEN a=b
530 PRINT:PRINT
540 :
550 h=(b-a)/n%
560 lo=FNa(a)/2
570 hi=FNa(b)/2
580 x=a
590 :
600 FOR j=1 TO n%-1
610 :   x=x+h
620 :   k=k+FNa(x)
630 NEXT
640 it=(lo+hi+k)*h
650 :
660 PRINT TAB(10)"Integral =";it
670 PRINT TAB(10)"----------";
680 FOR n=1 TO LEN(STR$(it)):PRINT"-";:NEXT
690 :
700 PRINT:PRINT:PRINT
710 INPUT "Another run (y/n)";y$
720 IF LEFT$(LOWER$(y$),1)="y" THEN RUN
730 CLS
740 END
750 :
760 :
770 REM Root found
780 PRINT"Root lies between:
790 PRINT
800 PRINT p1;" and ";p2
810 RETURN
820 :
830 :
840 REM Root not found
850 PRINT"Root not found after 40 iterations."
860 RETURN
870 :
880 :
890 REM Error routine
900 PRINT"Calculation cannot be performed on data"
910 PRINT"given."
920 PRINT
930 PRINT"Press any key to re-run program."
940 a$=INKEY$:IF a$="" THEN 940
950 RUN
```

P100 Simpson's Rule

Simpson's rule is rather more complicated than the trapezoidal rule. Here we use a quadratic curve, rather than a straight line, between the end points of the interval. This leads to the following rule:

$$\int_a^b f(x)\,dx \approx \left[\frac{h}{3}\ f(x_0) + 4f(x_1) + 2f(x_2) + 4f(x_3)\right.$$

$$\left. + 2f(x_4) +\ldots+ f(x_n)\right]$$

where $x_0 = a$, $x_n = b$ (n is even), $x_i = a + i * h$.

COMMANDS

Key in the program and RUN.
Enter the function as instructed.
Enter a and b when prompted.
Enter an even number of points as requested. If you enter an odd number, 1 will be added.

```
10 REM Simpson's rule
20 INK 0,1
30 INK 1,24
40 PAPER 0
50 PEN 1
60 BORDER 1
70 MODE 1
80 PRINT TAB(13)"SIMPSON'S RULE"
90 PRINT TAB(13)"+++++++++++++++"
100 PRINT:PRINT
110 PRINT"This   program   uses   Simpson's   rule"
120 PRINT"to evaluate a definite integral."
130 PRINT
140 PRINT "You are required to enter:"
150 PRINT
160 PRINT TAB(4)"1. Your function of x."
170 PRINT
180 PRINT TAB(4)"2. The range of values of x over"
190 PRINT TAB(7)"which you wish to value the"
200 PRINT TAB(7)"integral."
210 PRINT
220 PRINT TAB(4)"3. The number of sub-intervals"
230 PRINT TAB(7)"(this must be even).
240 PRINT:PRINT
250 PRINT"Press any key to continue."
```

```
260 a$=INKEY$:IF a$="" THEN 260
270 :
280 CLS
290 PRINT"To enter the function please type in:"
300 PRINT
310 PRINT"430 def fna(x)="
320 PRINT
330 PRINT"followed directly by the function,"
340 PRINT"then press the ENTER key.  When you"
350 PRINT"have done this, type in:"
360 PRINT
370 PRINT"run 430"
380 PRINT
390 PRINT"and then press the ENTER key again."
400 PRINT:PRINT:PRINT
410 STOP
420 :
430 REM This line is replaced by the function entered.
440 :
450 CLS
460 ON ERROR GOTO 970
470 INPUT "Lower value of x-range";a
480 PRINT
490 INPUT "Upper value of x-range";b
500 PRINT
510 INPUT "Number of points";n%
520 IF n%<4 THEN n%=4
530 IF n%-(INT(n%/2))*2<>0 THEN n%=n%+1
540 REM Above line ensures n% even.
550 IF a>b THEN a=b
560 PRINT:PRINT
570 :
580 h=(b-a)/n%
590 fi=FNa(a)/2
600 la=FNa(b)/2
610 x=a
620 :
630 FOR j=1 TO n%-3 STEP 2
640 :   x=x+h
650 :   od=od+FNa(x)
660 :   x=x+h
670 :   ev=ev+FNa(x)
680 NEXT
690 x=x+h
700 od=od+FNa(x)
710 it=(fi+la+4*od+2*ev)*h/3
720 :
730 PRINT TAB(10)"Integral =";it
740 PRINT TAB(10)"----------";
750 FOR n=1 TO LEN(STR$(it)):PRINT"-";:NEXT
760 :
770 PRINT:PRINT:PRINT
780 INPUT "Another run (y/n)";y$
790 IF LEFT$(LOWER$(y$),1)="y" THEN RUN
800 CLS
810 END
820 :
```

```
830 :
840 REM Root found
850 PRINT"Root lies between:
860 PRINT
870 PRINT p1;" and ";p2
880 RETURN
890 :
900 :
910 REM Root not found
920 PRINT"Root not found after 40 iterations."
930 RETURN
940 :
950 :
960 REM Error routine
970 PRINT"Calculation cannot be performed on data"
980 PRINT"given."
990 PRINT
1000 PRINT"Press any key to re-run program."
1010 a$=INKEY$:IF a$="" THEN 1010
1020 RUN
```

P101   The Last One

This program dissappears!

COMMANDS

Key in the program and RUN.

```
100 REM Program - The Last one
110 MODE 0
120 ORIGIN 0,0
130 FOR i=1 TO 200
140    c= i MOD 16
150    b1=i MOD 31:b2 =FIX(RND(TIME)*25)+1
160    BORDER b1,b2
170    MOVE i,i
180    DRAWR 0,400-2*i,c:DRAWR 640-2*i,0,c
190    DRAWR 0,2*i-400,c:DRAWR i*2-640,0,c
200    SOUND 1,i,10,15,0,0,0
210    SOUND 2,200-i,10,15,0,0,0
220    SOUND 3,FIX(RND(TIME)*200)+1,10,15,0,0,0
230 NEXT i
240 CALL 0
```